THE TYRANNY
OF RIGHTS

BREWSTER KNEEN

THE RAM'S HORN
OTTAWA, CANADA

Cover graphic: David Klein
Cover design: Matt Paquette
Editing and interior design: Cathleen Kneen

Library and Archives Canada Cataloguing in Publication

Kneen, Brewster
     The tyranny of rights / Brewster Kneen.

Includes bibliographical references and index.
ISBN 978-0-9813411-0-1

     1. Human rights. 2. Civil rights. I. Title.

JC571.K57 2009   323
C2009-905455-8

Published by The Ram's Horn, 2746 Cassels Street, Ottawa, ON, K2B 6N7, Canada.

Printed in Canada on FSC-certified paper.

Copies may be ordered direct from the publisher at a cost of $20 CDN, or via <www.ramshorn.ca>

ACKNOWLEDGMENTS

This book was not the result of divine revelation. It grew out of conversations and debate over a number of years with many colleagues and friends – far too many for me to name individually. I am grateful to all of them for their persistence and generosity. I must, however, specifically mention our indigenous Secwepemc neighbours when we lived in BC, who took us in and educated me in their traditional ways and attitudes.

I must also acknowledge the encouragement and stubborn criticism, along with the dedicated editorial work of Cathleen, my accomplice of these many years.

TABLE OF CONTENTS

INTRODUCTION: WHY TYRANNY?

The language of rights has been bothering me for a long time. It keeps cropping up and framing discussions: the right to food, for example; farmers' rights; intellectual property rights.

Rights are talked about as if they had some moral authority, while what they are actually about is law. Look at copyright, which is a type of legal protection for something like this book. It amounts to a form of exclusion, making it illegal for anyone else to copy my work – unless I choose to post it on the Internet and make it freely available, as I have with this book and others. So copyright can be seen as both a negative and a positive right before the law – positive for me, negative for you. (I am ignoring, for the moment, the place of publishers and libraries.) It does not, however, ensure that as a writer I get paid for my work.

As for food, human beings are no different than any other organism in requiring reliable nutrition to maintain life. Yet humans, I dare say, are the only organisms to come up with the idea of a right to food, which transforms a human necessity into a legal claim to be granted by some authority or other. There are no legal or governmental bodies for all the other organisms to appeal to for rights, including the right to food. People, or any other organisms, do not instinctively put themselves in a position of dependency on agencies and institutions – such as states and corporations – for their livelihood and nutrition. Yet claiming a right to food is exactly that.

It is a demand addressed to what is implicitly a superior power that might grant the claim – or not. It is not a political or social program for ensuring adequate nutrition. Furthermore, the recognition or granting of a right by a state does nothing, by itself, to give substance to the right. The right to food remains an empty bowl still to be filled.

Then there is the farmer's right to save seeds. To satisfy their nutritional needs, thousands of years ago people started selecting and saving the seeds of their favourite plants for planting next season – whether because they tasted better, or because they thrived under local conditions. This became a worldwide practice of subsistence peoples and continues today among peasant farmers as well as urban gardeners, without reference to state or juridical bodies. The strange idea of a *right* to save seeds amounts to a claim for an exemption from the wholesale appropriation and privatization of seeds by corporate entities.

As I noticed the increasing frequency of the language of rights in the statements of peasant movements and anti-poverty organizations, I realized that the language of rights and its assumption of individualism was increasingly displacing the cultural and linguistic concept and practice of 'responsibilities' and 'responsibility to care for others'.

Responsibility has to do with social relations. It is primarily a social and ethical practice, not a juridical concept. The replacement of responsibilities by rights has, however, served the wealthy and powerful well by providing an appearance of moral principle – right to life, right to food, right to land – while obscuring the lack of concrete action to

address the subject of the rights claim, thus leaving intact the
structures of power. A person, organization or state can
campaign hard to get a particular right recognized in an
international statement – including one from the United
Nations – without anyone having to actually do anything to
implement it. Indeed, rights are usually pursued precisely
because the state is violating the substance of the rights
claimed.

Despite the general assumption in the west that
individualism and the concept of rights are universal cultural
characteristics, most notably manifest by the United Nations'
Universal Declaration of Human Rights, neither the word
nor the concept of rights exist in the language and culture of
most of the world's people. This does not mean that indigenous peoples do not talk about rights when speaking English
or Spanish or French, but they do so because they need to
communicate with people who assume that the concept and
language of rights are universal cultural characteristics.

The way in which the cultural integrity of oppressed
or colonized peoples is deformed by using a language which
belongs to a colonizing culture, coupled with the power
assigned to the authority being petitioned to grant a right, is,
in my view, appropriately described as a tyranny.

It is, therefore, no mere provocation that I have titled
this book The Tyranny of Rights. With the increasing
presence, or even dominance, of the rights language in public
life and affairs of state, substantive issues of social justice
become marginalized while the language of rights masks
reality and imposes a linguistic and conceptual tyranny.

see Locke on Human Rights, the ~~core~~ heart and, in a way, the genesis of tyranny

A note about terminology

It is a challenge to come up with a single word or phrase to
refer such ill-defined concepts such as Enlightenment,

western or The West. Are we referring to Europe? Western Europe & North America? Australia and New Zealand? The cultures emanating out of this matrix – such as Spanish in South and Central America, French in Canada and the Carribean? Are we referring to territories or the people inhabiting them? When throughout the Americas the inhabitants are both aboriginal and of European and Asian heritage, who or what are we talking about? I have opted for ambiguity and the generic term 'western' without a capital 'w', which does not include aboriginal peoples per se, wherever they are, though there are numerous aboriginals who have chosen – or been compelled – to take on western identity.

While my major focus is on the concept and language of rights as understood and utilized in what I refer to as western culture, I will, I hope, give adequate recognition to the profoundly different culture and language of non-western peoples, including Indigenous Peoples.

THE GENESIS OF RIGHTS

It would be reasonable to argue that the concept of rights, including human rights, had its genesis two millennia ago in Greco-Roman civilizations. At that time, as lawyer Radha D'Souza points out, "the philosophical concept was associated with ethical and moral ideas of what is right or wrong. As all human beings are required to do right and abstain from doing wrong, the philosophical concept was supposed to guide people in 'right' actions."[1] In this con-text, 'rights' is about what it is right for people to do, or even their responsibility to do, as in 'doing good'.

The concept of 'rights' familiar to us today, however, arises from the particular culture of individualism, materialism and rationalism spawned by the European Enlightenment in the 18th century. This concept found its first full-blown public expression in the United Nations' Universal Declaration of Human Rights (UDHR) in 1948. Since then, and particularly in the past twenty years, the language of rights has come to assume a place of honour and utility in public discourse, in liberal as well as conservative politics, and among non-governmental organizations (NGOs) and civil society organizations (CSOs). Whether it be in reference to human rights or property rights, the right to life or abortion rights, farmers' rights, right to water or

or withheld can be given to anyone or anything – including corporations

also they

intellectual property rights, the word itself seems to have become a sort of essential – if powerless – invocation.

My argument is that 'rights' functions as code that identifies an idea, moral principle, or legal condition as a proxy for actualization of what is designated as a right.

Seldom is the actual meaning or content of 'a right' or 'rights' given, it being assumed, apparently, to be so universally recognized in natural law that no explanation or definition is required. The reasoning goes like this: Western Civilization is the most advanced form of human development; this civilization is founded on the principle of individual (personal) freedom, accompanied by the concepts of private property and the rights of property. The privileges of the individual (interpreted as rights) are, then, of supreme importance philosophically, politically and legally. The state (or society, as an organized and organic unit) is assigned the responsibility and power to implement and enforce these rights.

The consequence of this logic is that, politically, the claim of a right is framed as a demand, usually against the state, but its fulfilment remains an ephemeral goal since it remains up to the state (or dominant power) to give the right substantive meaning and content. It may, furthermore, not be in the state's interest to give meaning to any particular right, particularly when the state's interests are closely aligned with a particular class or sector of society, such as the corporate sector or financial elite. It all depends on whom the state represents and who actually exercises the power of the state. In any case, the supplicant is making an appeal to a higher power or authority, recognized as such by the appeal itself.

Sedgwick questions the author in context of basic needs

The most fundamental effect of the language of rights is that its adoption redefines moral-ethical issues of right, social justice and responsibility as legal issues. Violation of what is described as a right is regarded as a violation of a law, the breaking of a rule. Judith Shklar describes this as legalism: "The dislike of vague generalities, the preference for case-by-case treatment of all social issues, the structuring of all possible human relations into the form of claims and counter-claims under established rules, and the belief that the rules are 'there' – these combine to make up legalism as a social outlook."[2]

This shift is particularly problematic where implementation of judicial decisions is weak. Rights then become demands, or claims against others, without corresponding responsibilities to others. Beauchamp & Childress, in their classic text, *Principles of Biomedical Ethics*, comment that,

"It may seem odd that we have not employed the language of rights, especially in light of the recent explosion of rights language in contexts from applied ethics to foreign policy. Many moral controversies in biomedicine and public policy involve debates about rights, such as the right to die, a right to reproduce, a right of privacy, a right to life....These moral, political and legal debates sometimes appear to presuppose that no arguments or reasons can be persuasive unless they can be stated in the language of rights. Rights language is congenial to the liberal individualism pervasive in our society. At least since Thomas Hobbes, liberal individualists have employed the language of rights to buttress moral, social and political arguments and the Anglo-American legal tradition has incorporated this language."[3]

In the past two decades, the rights discourse has been ratcheted up to the international level, where not only NGOs but also governments demand the recognition of human rights. Now some states are even willing to intervene militarily in the name of protecting human rights, as in Afghanistan, Iraq, and Kosovo (in what was once Yugoslavia). At this point, great power politics takes over and the language of rights becomes simply a moralistic mask for the pursuit of power, as the sovereignty of the offending state is undermined or simply ignored, leaving it without authority to act on the rights claims and demands even if it wanted to.

To be sure, there are histories of struggles for justice, both personal and collective, carried out in the name of rights, though not necessarily human rights. The 1960s civil rights movement in the USA was, and was always called, 'the civil rights movement'. It sought, and eventually largely achieved, a substantial change in the structure of social (civil) relations in the USA, not just individual rights to be recognized as full and equal citizens. (It might even be described as an extra-legal class action against legalized white domination.) It is worth noting that, as a movement for rights, it started not when some lawyer pleaded before a white court a case for the right of blacks to sit at the front of the bus, but when Rosa Parks, trained in non-violent direct action at Highlander Folk School, decided to sit down in the front of the bus in Birmingham, Alabama, in 1955.

While the civil rights movement did achieve a vast increase in social justice, it did not end racial discrimination in the USA (as President Obama has noted), nor did it address class structure, and some of the individuals and organizations that were major players in that struggle have since become distressingly right-wing politically.[4] One has to wonder if a lack of discernment between individual and social rights, and rights and justice, allowed for this unfortunate shift.

A contrasting situation might be found in Latin America where social rights have a long history, particularly in the Christian churches, and are assumed as an aspect of the fabric of social life, at least for the 'white' or European settlers, if not for indigenous peoples. The notion of rights, social or individual, is actually alien to the indigenous peoples of the Americas, North as well as South, as I will discuss later. For indigenous peoples, and, as I have discovered, most non-

Europeans, 'responsibility for others' occupies the space that
'my rights' occupies for the children of the Enlightenment. (I
will return to this later.)

My conclusion is that social and individual justice is
not furthered by the language of rights. Justice would be
better served not by making claims and demands, but by
stating what is being done and must be done by those that
otherwise might be making a claim for the right to do
something. The following statement of a meeting of
indigenous people from autonomous communities in Mexico
in 2003 expresses this well:

"The government resolved not to recognize our
fundamental rights in the Constitution, but to
intensify its plundering, destruction and robbery
policies towards our lands, territories and natural
resources. ... Confronted with the aforementioned, we
have decided to stop demanding further recognition
for the exercises of our own rights, so now we demand
respect for our lands, territories and autonomy. We
have resolved that if this State has lost its legitimacy, by
its legal practices, we must exercise our autonomy *de
facto*, thus addressing our grave situation and looking
forward to a better future for our children."[5]

It is time to consider whether the language of rights
actually serves the intents of social justice or has become just
an illusion of intent – good intent, to be sure – behind which
individualization and privatization is carried on unimpeded.

THE INDIVIDUALISM OF RIGHTS

The corrosive philosophy of rights has eaten its way into the individualistic minds of westerners so thoroughly that the majority of people appear to be convinced that recognition of the social dimension of life, indeed, any suggestion of the legitimacy let alone necessity of collective identity and authority, can only be at the expense of individual identity and freedom. The rights, liberties and freedom of the individual are set against the claims and even existence of a society or social order. There is no recognition of, or place for, either responsibilities or obligations to society, the state or, indeed, any collective authority, except that which advances personal interests. For example, tax evasion, both personal and corporate, is widely engaged in and not generally considered as anti-social and criminal. Naturally, any idea of public or public good disappears along the way.

Yet at the same time, rights advocates everywhere consistently regard the state as the agency that must take responsibility for ensuring that human rights are respected and observed. More than that, they appear to assume that the state is on their side – or at least could be if they can muster the right language and approach. Beneath this lies an enduring faith in liberal democracy, even to the point of being considered the only legitimate form of government.

For example, The International Centre for Human Rights and Democratic Development (Rights & Democracy) has denounced chronic hunger in Haiti as a human rights violation, but not a crime, saying that "existing policies are failing to alleviate chronic hunger in Haiti.... While the burden of responsibility for addressing these issues rests with the Government of Haiti and its agencies ... Haiti's international donors, including Canada, must also take immediate steps to address food shortages in the country.... Only policies based on the human right to food can provide the sustainable solutions to the chronic food insecurity that Haitians are facing today."[6] Unfortunately, Rights & Democracy, like many others, does not appear to explain just what policies, laws, political changes or actions will actually translate this right to food into real nutrition for the people. Nor do they explain why "international donors ... must also take immediate steps ..." Nor do they make a practice of identifying, at least publicly, the political and military interventions that may have been contributing factors to the Haitian tragedy.*[7]

The sad decline of cooperatives in North America and their conversion into capitalist enterprises appealing to individual benefits rather than collective good, can in part be

Points to failure of collective action v. climate change see /p.8

* In 1991 a military coup overthrew the first democratically elected president of Haiti, Jean-Bertrand Aristide, after the first President Bush had devoted substantial effort to undermine it and prepare the grounds for a military coup. The USA then instantly supported the military junta and its wealthy supporters for the benefit of US businesses. By 1995, Washington felt that the destruction of Haiti had proceeded long enough and President Clinton sent the Marines in to topple the junta and restore the elected government. The restored government, however, was compelled to accept a harsh neoliberal program, with no barriers to US-dominated export and investment.[7]

attributed to the individualism of western culture. This 'rugged individualism' does not, however, explain the contradiction between libertarian philosophy* and respect for and participation in the military, an authoritarian institution which deliberately fosters a team mentality and collective action combined with an appeal to the glory of individual 'sacrifice' in the service of the state.**

The individualism of the rights argument finds extreme expression in the absurd notion of foetal rights – the assertion that a foetus, assigned the status of an individual person, has rights over against its mother, who is its social as well as physical context and life support. Ultra-sound imaging contributes to this notion of the foetus as an autonomous person by isolating the image from its context, making it appear as if it were not utterly dependent on its mother. A profound alienation of infant from mother can all too easily result. Women have been taken to court and jailed for 'abusing' the baby they were carrying, and there have even been cases of parents being sued by their own disabled children for 'wrongful birth'. This extreme alienation, or

---

* Libertarian: a political philosophy that places supreme value on individual 'freedom' ahead of any social or collective identity or responsibility or any claims by the state. There are both right wing and left wing expressions of libertarianism. The right-wing version finds expression in North American populism and many fundamentalist religious sects, while on the left, communal and communitarian philosophies, in close association with anarchism, may exhibit both a distrust of state authority and a strong sense of personal and communal responsibility.

** Every time a Canadian soldier is killed in Afghanistan there is a paean of praise for his or her heroism all over the corporate press, crowding out any doubts about the purpose or legitimacy of the Canadian presence in Afghanistan.

disconnectedness, also finds expression in wide-spread alienation from Creation or Mother Earth.

This libertarian thinking sees freedom or liberty only in the autonomy of the individual – a kind of exceptionalism in which a person understands their life, together with their needs and desires, to be quite independent of the society in which they live, rather than contingent on it. The desires and demands of the individual take precedence over or ignore the welfare of the community.

A good example of this mentality was expressed by the Ottawa dentist who wanted to put up a temporary plastic shelter for his car at the end of his driveway, in front of his house, so he would not have to shovel the snow from his driveway. His argument against the city bylaw limiting such neighbourhood eyesores was that the plastic shelter would reduce his chance of having a heart attack from shoveling snow. He intended to challenge the city under the Canadian Charter of Rights and Freedoms "to defend what I see as a right to protect my health and safety at home."[8]

A similar outlook was provided by an Ottawa newspaper columnist in commenting on a new city bylaw restricting the cutting of mature trees in the city. "City Hall has just appropriated your right to do what you see fit with your big, old tree. ... Perhaps because we've lived in the Nanny State so long, we don't even blink when Nanny walks away with our God-given chainsaws. ... It's either my stinking tree or it isn't."[9] The fact that the tree on 'his property' was probably there long before he became owner of the property, would still be there after he was gone, and was part of a complex eco- and social system far bigger than himself and his yard is apparently irrelevant, or simply not understood.

Unfortunately, contemporary medical and bio-ethics have been constructed on the principle of the autonomy of the individual with little if any regard for the social context and the health of the society as a whole.*[10] Thus acute care for the individual in need preempts public health care and preventive medicine. Nor is there appreciable room in medical practice for consideration of environmental or workplace causes of disease and illness. It is far more profitable for the drug companies to push drugs to treat individuals (as long as the 'patient' group is large enough to provide adequate profit or can be expanded by identifying and naming new 'diseases' for treatment, a practice referred to as 'disease mongering' by its critics) than to explore and address social and environmental causes of illness.

When Québec Liberal Leader Jean Charest said he wants to give "a couple that wants children ... all the help possible" and that he plans to allocate $35-million a year to cover costs of in-vitro fertilization, epidemiologist Abby Lippman commented that if he were really concerned about a low birth rate he should tackle its systemic reasons instead of trying to buy 'motherhood' votes by funding technologies for individual couples that remain insufficiently regulated and monitored.

---

* The aborted campaign by former US President George W. Bush to transform the US Social Security system into an individual investment program was a direct attack on the concept of social solidarity and its replacement with individualism-via-ownership. "Founded on principles of general solidarity and publicly shared risk, social security is the most important part of what remains of the US social protection system ... Objections [to the Bush program] and counter-proposals assume that the Bush administration is concerned with making social security more viable. But the primary goal is different: to undermine commitment to the logic of citizen solidarity and public risk management. In the words of Bush: "If you own something, you have a vital stake in the future of our country. The more ownership there is in America, the more vitality in America, and the more people have a vital stake in the future of this country."[9]

"Addressing systemic determinants of a low birth rate would commit him, for example, to removing environmental risks to fertility, guaranteeing working conditions and first-rate daycare programs that permit women to balance paid and unpaid work, allowing women to have early and comprehensive access to care from primary health-care providers, and ensuring the basic income and housing conditions needed for the health of parents and their children."[11]

As should be clear by now, my argument is that designating something as a right reduces it to an individual claim, thereby reducing social solidarity, communal identity and appreciation of the public good. It becomes a matter of the individual, even in the form of a corporation, making claims against the state and asking or demanding that the state recognize these claims. Thus, while a person may appeal on the grounds of human rights for limitations of the power of the state to arbitrarily detain a citizen as a 'security threat'. the state may deny the human rights argument in the name of public security, that is, the security of the state, which in the current state of affairs may mean corporate security. At the same time, a corporation or its lobby organization will demand that the state grant it, by means of licensing, the right to pollute (as is the case with pulp mills, mining operations and oil field/tar sands activity) while it ignores the extra-legal activities of the corporation in dealing with public opposition to its activities. It's all a question of who has the power. With the state (by which I mean national, provincial/state or local government) recognized as the only institutional expression of the public, it is thus called upon to play quite contradictory roles.*

There is, then, not only no *public*, but also no *citizen* in the sense of socially conscious public person. The

---

*see Rights and the State, page 40

public is, consequently, reconstructed in the form of focus groups of carefully selected individuals and of individuals representing special interests and identified as 'stakeholders'. The cult of the individual is also blatantly manifest in the business press, giving the impression that the rise or fall of corporations is solely dependent on the personal abilities of their chief executive, even though it is obvious that an executive without office staff is dysfunctional, to say nothing of a factory without workers, despite the fact that the workers are paid only a very small percentage of what the executive claims as his due – or right!

The advocacy and pursuit of rights, both individual and corporate, is consequently bound to fragment a society into competing interests (echoes of class struggle), destroying any sense of solidarity and ultimately, destroying the very fabric of society itself.

"This then is the crux of the matter. The discourse of human rights serves as an instrument for the pathological expansion of modern and postmodern liberalism and what accompanies it: free market capitalism."[12]

THE RISE OF RIGHTS
AS DOMINANT DISCOURSE

The founding of the United Nations in 1945 and the proclamation of the United Nations' Universal Declaration of Human Rights in 1948 may not have created the discourse of human rights, but they did lay an apparently altruistic or even idealistic foundation for the emergence of the language of rights at the centre of liberal democratic political activity. The context of this was, of course, the extreme destruction of World War II and the Nazi program of human extermination, which overshadowed the killing and destruction carried out by the Allies, such as the bombing of Dresden, Hiroshima and Nagasaki.

The appropriate response should have been the creation of a genuinely supra-national authority with the power to enforce disarmament and to intervene, when requested, with peacekeeping forces to halt war-making. Instead, the idealism of the period was captured by the language of universal human rights and the provision of a seat and a vote for every sovereign state in the UN General Assembly. But while the United Nations was ostensibly a global body, it was in fact a European-North American project, designed to protect and further the political and economic interests of capital and the liberal democratic states. The reigning holy trinity was Human Rights, Liberal Democracy and Capitalism (later referred to politely as 'market economy'). Countries outside this realm may have been present in the UN, but their informally assigned role was that of observers and policy ratifiers, not policy creators. The Soviet Union may have been a permanent member of the Security Council, but the other four permanent members were France, the United Kingdom, the United States of America and Nationalist China*, all decidedly capitalist states aligned against the Soviet Union. The UN itself was physically located in the USA, not in Switzerland, a neutral nation which had been the site of the UN's unfortunate predecessor, the League of Nations.

Richard Falk, an emeritus professor of international law appointed in 2008 by the United Nations Human Rights Commission as a Special Rapporteur on 'the situation of human rights' in the Palestinian territories under Israeli occupation, provided a much starker description of the power arrangements of the United Nations. He describes the UN as regulatory law for the weak and impunity for the strong.

> "It is the weak, the leaders of the Third World countries, who are subject to this legal framework of the United Nations. The strong are exempt, and that goes back to the end of the Second World War. US military people were not prosecuted for using the atomic bomb in Hiroshima and Nagasaki, while the Japanese and the Germans were held responsible for war

---

* 'Nationalist China' refers to the Chiang Kai-shek dictatorship that was driven out of China and migrated to Taiwan in 1949. The USA was steadfast in its recognition of Chiang Kai-shek's government as the legitimate government of all China. In 1971 the UN recognized the communist government of mainland China as the legitimate government of the country and thus occupier of the Security Council seat.

crimes.... International life ... is characterized by
pervasive double standards. It goes back to the UN
Charter itself, which gives the five permanent members of the Security Council a veto. And that veto, in
effect, is saying that the UN Charter and international law do not apply to the powerful. The
charter is a regulatory framework for the weak .. The
strong have impunity and exemption."[13]

As for the rest of the world, it was largely divided
into 'developing' or 'under-developed', the assumption being that history had a unique trajectory best illustrated by
the development of the United States of America. The
policies of the United States assumed the authority of
natural law, and accordingly the United States assumed
responsibility for ensuring, by one means or the other, the
development of the less fortunate countries of the world.
The Soviet realm was doomed to fail, and the USA and its
allies would help its fledgling empire crumble under the
weight of the arms race and the empty promises of
capitalism.

After its founding, it took three years for the UN to
agree on the non-binding Universal Declaration of Human
Rights (UDHR) and another eighteen years – until 1966 –
for the Declaration to be translated into two binding
international treaties or Covenants. It finally took on the
force of international law in 1976 after being ratified by a
sufficient number of individual nations. The rights
enumerated in the UDHR had been split into the International Covenant on Civil and Political Rights, with the
premise that these rights were individual in nature and,
presumably, not threatening to the character of the capitalist
state itself, and the International Covenant on Economic,
Social and Cultural Rights, which recognizes social or
collective rights. "The West was the champion of individual
civil and political rights.... The East, led by the Soviet

Union, was more inclined to support economic, social and cultural rights of the collective, arguing that civil and political rights were capitalist concepts."[14]

An underlying anomaly is that "unlike the general case of international law [which regulates] the conduct of states vis-à-vis other states, international human rights law regulates the conduct of states vis-à-vis individuals because human rights belong to individuals not states."[15] I must note here that corporations were never mentioned as subjects of human rights, although they are granted the legal status of persons, that is, they are recognized in western law as 'artificial persons'.

It is therefore ironic that power in the United Nations, at least on rights issues, is now shifting from the West to the rest. According to a study by the European Council on Foreign Relations published in September 2008, the West's efforts to use the United Nations to promote its values and shape the global agenda are failing as a result of its losing the power to set the rules. "The pattern of votes in the General Assembly shows opposition to the European Union is growing, spurred by a common resistance to European efforts at promoting universal human rights, with the agenda increasingly being shaped by China, Russia and their allies. A decade ago European rights policies had the support of 72% of UN members, but in 2007 only 48%. Support for the US dropped from 77% to 30%."[16] China and Russia, which publicly defend national sovereignty and non- intervention in sovereign countries (which has not always characterized their actual behaviour), have been the primary beneficiaries of this shift.

While power in the UN may be shifting internally, the UDHR has performed according to intent and since the 1960s there has been a continuous advance in the use of the language and politics of rights in the western 'market democracies'. In addition, rights are now being widely *but what of those beings who are outside of any claim of having rights (is the integrity of beings only possible within an anthropocentric framework.*

claimed not only by and for non-human persons (corporations) as well as human persons and collectives and animals, but more recently for plants, trees and nature itself.

Theologian Esther Reed offers a cogent argument for the rise of the language of rights: "After World War II, and in the absence of unifying political ideologies or religious belief systems to bind the vast majority of individuals together, human rights gained force as a source of ethical value in and of themselves.... Regardless of disputed foundations and interpretations, human rights function increasingly to provide a transcultural and normative discourse under which international affairs can be conducted and global commerce regulated."[17]

In the early 1970s, the language of human rights was used strategically by Latin American socialists, accompanied by a virtual disappearance of progressive political positions and programs. A Brazilian offered the explanation at the time that the language of rights was the only language of resistance that socialists could use that would not immediately make them a target of the military dictatorships then taking control in Latin America.*[18] A call for the observance of human rights – including the abstract 'right to life' – was far more audible to the liberal democrats in the north and their business interests than a call for condemnation of, and legal action against, the murderous dictators. Human rights are understood, correctly, to be an issue of how individuals are treated, while a dictatorship is a structural affair. Condemning a dictatorship could well have far more deleterious effects on corporate interests than

---

* "Human rights today represent the universal language in which global relations can be normatively regulated. In Asia, Africa and South America, they constitute the sole language in which the opponents and victims of murderous regimes and civil wars can raise their voices against violence, repression, and persecution, and against violations of their human dignity."[17]

C. U. Wttmass cntch 22.

calling for recognition and implementation of human rights – while the structures of oppression and exploitation continue.

While it was clearly necessary at that time for leftists of whatever stripe to avoid calling attention to their political position, there is also a long tradition in Latin America of advocacy for social justice, particularly by the progressive sector of the Catholic Church; so while issues of human rights were raised, they were within a framework of social justice, as well as to stop the murders and disappearances of opponents of the dictatorships. The rights claimed were not property rights, but social rights against the claims of property, i.e., the power and impunity of the wealthy elite and the latifundistas.

It may have been natural, expedient and wise to employ the language of rights in those circumstances, but the act of addressing the state (one's own or others) with demands and claims for recognition and implementation of human rights implicitly gives recognition to the authority – if not legitimacy – of the state. The state, as I have already noted, may easily and formally recognize the rights demanded without relinquishing any of its power and without actually ensuring that the material preconditions of these rights are in place. As David Harvey puts it, "rights cluster around two dominant logics of power – that of the territorial state and that of capital. However much we might wish rights to be universal, it is the state that has to enforce them. If political power is not willing, then notions of rights remain empty."[19]

I should clarify here the distinction I make between justice and rights. Justice is often used in reference to law, as in 'bring to justice' or 'justice is done'. It implies an action actually accomplished, and the law is assumed to be 'just', that is, fair and without bias towards one class, race, gender, religion or appearance. It is also assumed that the judiciary functions independently of the state, even though appointed by the state. The image of Justice as a robed, blindfolded figure holding a balance, the scales of justice, is very revealing. Justice, we can say, is without content, the content being provided by the specifics of a case brought before the courts. More colloquially, we might say that an action (or institution) is just, meaning that it is fair to all the parties concerned. What is meant by justice or just, then, depends on the context and what those involved consider to be just and right. Rights, on the other hand, do not imply action. They are statements of what are considered to be desirable conditions with the added attribute of being moral, with its implication of being in tune with or expressions of natural law. Casting rights in the language of law shifts responsibility for achievement, or enforcement, from persons to the state.

Like progressive movements in Latin America for many decades, Indigenous Peoples, north and south, have made many declarations calling for recognition of their rights as Indigenous Peoples. The rights language is often oddly out of place and appears to have been inserted in the text – or perhaps the whole text has been prepared – to appeal to northern 'white' funding agencies and governments in language they are more comfortable with. In making such appeals, there is indeed a recognition of existing power and wealth relations, but framing appeals in the language of rights adds legitimacy to the power of the oppressing culture.

The establishment of collective or communal rights ('aboriginal title and rights') over their territorial biodiversity and traditional knowledge has been pursued by a variety of Indigenous peoples and groupings. What seemed at first to be a way to control the appropriation of 'genetic resources' (plants, seeds, human DNA), along with the knowledge of their use, by drug companies and opportunistic individuals has turned out to be just the opposite, entangling the people of one culture in the rights nets of another. The corporate lawyers enjoy virtually unlimited financial backing, while demanding that Indigenous peoples play by the same rules, but without the financial resources. Justice is not done. This has left many Indigenous peoples with little alternative but secrecy and territorial defense. On top of this is the contradiction of appealing to the state for recognition of communal or collective 'rights' when rights themselves are individualistic.

As seen in Mexico and elsewhere, including Canada (after decades of fruitless treaty negotiations), some Indigenous peoples, as peoples, not individuals, have come to understand this contradiction and taken matters into their own hands. All too often this has triggered a repressive, if not deadly, response from the state.

The following declaration from the Indigenous National Congress, Central Pacific Region of Mexico, is a very strong statement of autonomy, strength and intent beyond rights:

"[T]he armed uprising of the Zapatista National Liberation Army in 1994 represents a historical dividing line in our people's long raid and fight for our complete liberation: together we created a movement that overwhelmed the Nation and the world, seeking the constitutional recognition of our rights through the incorporation of the San Andrés Agreements into the National Constitution.

"The betrayal of all the Mexican Government Institutions in 2001, approving, passing and ratifying the Indigenous Counter Reform, known as the "Barttlet-Cevallos-Ortega" Law, compelled us to reject the application of such Reformation and to declare the San Andrés Agreements as our people's Constitution in indigenous matters, calling all the indian people of

Mexico not to seek recognition from the state any more and strengthen, by action, our autonomy, our own government and our culture....

"With the intention of fortifying the autonomy of our communities we appeal [sic] to:

1. Defend the lands, the territories, the hills, the waters, the spiritual and natural beings as well as our own knowledge and culture.

2. Fortify our own government, our assemblies and our traditional and rural authorities under the principle of 'to rule obeying' (*el principio de mandar obedeciendo*).

3. Preserve our own maizes by sowing, in order to guarantee our food sovereignty ...

4. Guard our traditional medicine ...."[20]

THE FALSE ASSUMPTION OF
UNIVERSALITY

The concept and language of rights is deeply and uniquely rooted in western history and culture. It expresses the western self-understanding that it is a universal culture, if not fully recognized and accepted as such yet, then on its way to being so. As I have explained, rights is a legal concept, so it is helpful to consider Timothy Mitchell's explanation of how the western concept of law became universal since the same thing could be said of rights. "Modern government, like modern science, the European believed, was based on principles true in every country. Its strength lay in its universalism."[21]

> "How is the general character of law produced? How do the rules of property achieve the quality of being universal? There is no straightforward answer to this question. Modern jurisprudence sees law as self-establishing, existing as a system of rules whose validity is established only by other rules.... In the positive accounts of law and economics, the genealogy of what is taken to be a universal system of rules is not open to investigation. This is inevitable, for if the axiomatic

had its origins in particular histories and political acts, its claim to universalism would be lost."[22]

The imperial, universal identity of rights is proclaimed by the UDHR and reinforced with various subsequent UN declarations, such as the 1986 Declaration on the Right to Development which presumes that there is a common, agreed upon definition of development and therefore offers none – another expression of western universalism.

There are, however, a great many languages and peoples for whom the notion of rights is simply non-existent. In many languages (among them Algonquin, Aymara, Bangla, Basque, Khmer, Korean, Japanese, Quechua, Turkish, Shuswap/Secwepemc ...) there is simply no word for rights, or at least there was none until the concept of rights was imported from western cultures and a word for rights had to be created.

Marcelo Saavedra-Vargas, an Indigenous Aymara from Bolivia, told me, for example, that the notion of rights does not really exist in Andean philosophy. "Rather, we have other notions that talk about our existences as integral parts of a dynamic set of relationships and responsibilities. For instance, *Suma Qamaña*, which sort of translates into 'living and coexisting well' – living well among our fellow menwomen (*chachawarmi*) and coexisting harmoniously with other sentient beings, such as animals, plants, rivers, mountains and other beings that are harder to sense with our crude human senses."[23]

If the language of rights is not universal, what takes its place is the language of responsibility. If the individualism of rights is not universal, what takes its place is the social being who lives not a solitary existence but a socially enmeshed life.

I have tried to capture this in the following diagram:

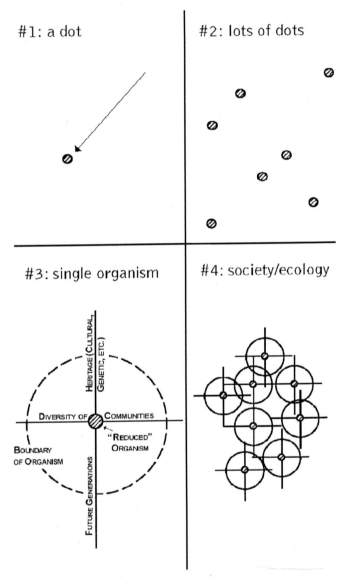

This depicts the western individual as a dot, and society as a collectivity or aggregate of dots – lots of dots.

Society, however, is actually made up of social beings in a matrix of relations, backward and forward in time, laterally in the present. The individual then identifies him or herself in a web or fabric of relationships. What I mean by forward and backward in time is that no one lives simply in the present. We have our own history, shaped by many people and experiences. As I am to-day, I think of myself as being made up not only of my blood forebears but of the many people who have shaped my life as well as the experiences I have had. I also know that as I have gone through life I have, in turn, left bits of me along the way and contributed to the lives and experiences of others. Similarly, in the present I am part of a visible community, not only that I see about me, but that I am part of around the world. These 'lateral' relations include not just humans, but all kinds of non-humans as well. In a real sense, I know that 'all my relations' includes a vast array of humans and non-humans.

The claim of universality of the rights language and concept, then, like the universality of western law, has to be reconsidered. If there is any language in which there is no word for rights, the claim of universality of the concept obviously does not hold.

In Bangla, the language of Bangladesh, there was no word for rights. The word *Hoque* was created to translate the word rights, and it refers to 'collective responsibility to care for others', as well as 'truth'. Farhad Mazhar, a leader of Nayakrishi Andolon (New Agricultural Movement) in Bangladesh, offers an eloquent description of this:

"Any discourse of 'rights' presupposes an autonomous and egocentric subject. In contrast, Nayakrishi Andolon is concerned not with 'persons' or fictitious subjects endowed with 'rights', who exist outside society or the community, but with 'relations'.... Nayakrishi is critical of organizing society around egocentric assertions and privileging the individual over and against the community or nature....

"Interestingly, in the Bangla language we do not have any word like 'rights' – it is translated as *odhikar*, which is Sanskrit, rather than Bangla.... While we had no word for rights, we have words such as *daiy* (obligation) and *daya* (caring for the other) and, taking into account other historical, anthropological and cultural data, we concluded that the culture we inherit gives greater importance to our obligation to care for others than to rights. But we have a problem too, for the caring and the obligations towards others could also become oppressive if it is reduced to a mechanical and lifeless relation.

"... So the dominant discourses of rights create serious problems for Nayakrishi Andolon. Its intimate corollary – obligations and responsibility – is also a problematic area, since it articulates the deficit in the original notion of rights in order to retain the privleged position of rights. This is the reason why obligations and responsibility are not posited first as independent of rights, but only in conjunction with rights, for example in the phrase 'rights and responsibilities'. In contrast, Nayakrishi would like to explore the relation of obligation to the other – human beings and the non-human world – in order to experience real joy in life and in order to create the possibility of a post-imperial and post-capitalist global order ... "[24]

North American Algonquins have no word in their language for rights: "Our laws do not involve a concept of rights. In our cultures, mutual respect and benefit are understood as imperatives for survival. Aboriginal cultures regard law as a complex set of responsibilities to the land and in human relations."[25]

Cyril Powles, a missionary teaching in Japan for much of his life, told me that "Japan had no word for rights up to the 19th century when contact with the West forced them to coin one – the word *kenri* – which is a mishmash of 'authority/power' and 'advantage'– and until relatively recently in most quarters it was considered to be a synonym for selfishness, responsibility being the only truly good value."

A Korean scholar, Kim Yong-Bock, wrote from Seoul to say that in Korean, 'right' (*Kwon-Ri*) indicates legal right. It is a combination of two characters: power + interest, and is likely a translation of the Western concept. It is, not surprisingly, very close to the Japanese words in meaning. Yong-Bock's further explanation indicates how important it is to understand the cultural and historical context of what might seem to be simple contemporary terms. In East Asia, he wrote, "any right should be grounded in the Mandate of Heaven, which is the foundation of all legal authority of the state or ruler."

"The Mandate of Heaven (*Pi-nyi-n: Tia-nmìng*) is a traditional Chinese philosophical concept concerning the legitimacy of rulers. Heaven would bless the authority of a just ruler, but would be displeased with a despotic ruler and would withdraw its mandate. The Mandate of Heaven would then transfer to those who would rule best.

"The Mandate of Heaven was a well-accepted idea among the common people of China, as it argued for the removal of incompetent or despotic rulers, and provided an incentive for rulers to rule well and justly. The concept was often invoked by philosophers and scholars in ancient China as a way to curtail the abuse of power by the political rulers.

"The Mandate of Heaven had no time limitations, instead depending on the just and able performance of the ruler. When people were resisting an oppressive ruler, they would use the slogan *Minshim Chonshim* (the people are heaven). And, of course, kings in China, Japan and Korea went to great lengths to prove that they had the heavenly mandate."

Turkish professor Mustafa Koç explained that, in Turkish 'right' is translated as '*hak*'. "It is originally an Arabic word and has multiple meanings. *Hak* (with a capital) means the God. *Hak* also means justice, fairness, share, mercy, truth, and in our current useage it is also used as 'right'. In the Ottoman system, land was not privately owned, but usufruct rights were granted to families as long as they continue to till the land. Modern Turkey adopted Swiss civil law and Italian criminal Law in 1926 and right as a form of entitlement was introduced (albeit not clearly understood) at that time."[26]

Another Turkish professor elaborated: "In Turkish *hak* is 'right' in the sense that you can claim and possess *hak*. In Turkish (and as far as I know in Arabic) *hak* and *adalet* (justice) are often mentioned together. A derivative of *hak* in Turkish, *haksiz* (the suffix, *siz*, meaning without), means unjust. Justice and being just are highly valued in Islamic tradition, and a believer's duty is to see that everyone gets his/her *hak* so justice can be done. In other words, rights and justice are connected, but instead of itemization of one's rights, there is a tendency to specify one's corollary duties (e.g., do not kill infants – as opposed to the right to live; or give orphans their share – as opposed to the right to property)."[27]

Marcelo Saavedra-Vargas elaborated:

"The UDHR has been integrated into national constitutions that have been imposed on our nations and countries, as in Bolivia and Ecuador. These legal charters have been instrumental in the formation and transformation of national states, most of the times overriding our [Indigenous persons'] deep beliefs and ethos. And, of course, the building blocks of these constitutions come about through the pervasive (and sometimes perverse) notion of individual rights and an erroneous and arrogant conception of 'development'. The imposition of the Western cosmovision has happened completely disrespectfully of the Other."[28]

Alain Gresh, in an essay titled "The West's selective reading of history," discusses the historical genesis of what he refers to as "the Manichean view of history as an eternal confrontation between civilisation and barbarism" that seems to shape western consciousness and, to some extent at least, account for this assumption of universalism. As Gresh explains it, this universalism extends only to the societies considered civilized – the 'dark' barbarians do not count. The societies recognized as civilized "could all distinguish freedom from slavery, and they were all committed broadly to what we today would identify as an individualistic view of humanity."[29]

The universality attributed to the idea of human rights appears to be more a projection of arrogance and imperial intent than a description of reality. As Ziauddin Sardar succinctly puts it,

"...there is no such thing as universal human rights; there is merely a practice that has been abstracted from the ideas of one culture and termed universal.... The UN Declaration of Human Rights assumes a universal human nature common to all peoples. It further assumes that this human nature is knowable and that it is known by a universal organ of knowledge: human reason.... Other forms of life are inferior to humans and have no rights."[30]

The individualism of rights will not be redeemed by talking about collective rights. The idea of rights can only be associated with the singularity of a dot, as in my diagram, or an aggregate of dots. It cannot relate to a person who understands him or herself in terms of relationships to others and the world about them, or a society that understands itself as a web or fabric of life.

"Since an autonomous, isolated individual does not exist in non-western cultures and traditions, it does not make sense to talk of his or her rights; and where there are no rights, it is quite absurd to speak of their denial or annulment. However ... notions of the individual's dignity and the respect that is due to it exist in all non-western cultures...."[31]

The only reference to a social right in what is now described as the Bill of Rights in the United States (the first ten amendments to the Constitution of the USA) is the simple: "right of the people peaceably to assemble".*

Similarly, the only words in the Canadian Charter of Rights and Freedoms that suggest any form of collective rights are "freedom of peaceful assembly" and "freedom of association" – in other words, the freedom of individuals to gather with other individuals, whether in the town square, the union hall or school gym (but not the privately-owned shopping mall), though the acceptability of such gatherings is limited by the subjective and problematic condition of 'peaceful'. If the Charter is regarded as a tool to protect citizens from the state, at whatever level, the implication is that people gathering together may well constitute a threat to the state. This whole dynamic would be ridiculous if the state were actually a democracy controlled by the citizens and only makes sense if you regard citizens as lots of dots and not a society.

---

* In the USA there is the odd political claim of 'states' rights' against the federal government which is analogous to the rights claims of individuals against the state.

RIGHTS: NATURAL AND DIVINE

The idea and language of rights, particularly human rights, has become commonplace among both secular and religious constituencies. Its authority in the eyes and ears of those using it is unquestioned, yet the source of its authority, like that of law, remains largely unarticulated, as discussed in the last chapter. Human rights may be assumed to be inherent in the being of a person, i.e., *natural* or *ontological,* with the authority of *natural law,* but this begs the question of authority: who or what defines the law and enforces it, and what is the source of this authority?

The assertion of rights assumes an opposition: rights is a claim *against,* an attempt to limit *power over* or a demand for the space in which to act or the authority to do so. Without a real life context, a right is a meaningless abstraction. One may wish to claim *natural* rights; but to have meaning, rights have to be recognized, granted and implemented, but by whom or what? *God-given* or *natural,* rights require a sponsor or source. To be functional, they have to have legal and/or moral authority and be implemented in the real world. What bridges the gap or translates the meaning between God-given and natural? The logic of rights requires that some power, class, institution or structure has first to recognize and then have the means to fulfill the expectations or demands of rights. Those with the power to do so can, however, simply proclaim and exploit rights, as is the current practice of corporations in regard to property, labour and 'genetic resources'. The claims of rights by the less powerful, on the other hand, have to be argued in the courts of the dominant power, which means from a position of weakness.

In the secular Enlightenment tradition, a right refers to a license, allowance, privilege or exception granted by a secular state power. The idea of a secular, or natural, right itself arose out of the religious doctrine of the 'divine right of kings' with its hierarchical cosmology, but when the religious authority claimed by or attributed to the king and the church was secularized in the course of the Enlightenment, the privilege of granting rights passed from divinely-empowered king and church to the state. (The French Revolution of 1789-1799 epitomizes this.) The secular state then became the quasi-religious source and guarantor of both human and property rights, even though, theoretically, the state was simply recognizing natural rights.

In a religious or spiritual context, humans may be understood as the children of Pachamama (Mother Earth) or the Creator who gives the Instructions as to what it is to be human. In the Christian faith, the *human* is theologically defined as 'created in the image of God' and therefore commanding respect and responsible for exercising authority.

The preamble of the United States Declaration of Independence (July 4, 1776), attributed to Thomas Jefferson, expresses the ambiguous nature of rights in the terms 'self-evident' and 'endowed by their Creator': "We hold these truths to be self-evident, that all men [sic] are created equal, that they are endowed by their Creator with certain unalienable Rights, that among these are Life, Liberty and the pursuit of Happiness." These words not only strongly express the individualism of the rights language, but also suggest an ideological, rather than legal, predisposition: it is hard to imagine the wording of a legal claim to the right of happiness, much less the definition of happiness itself, (although the drug industry might be willing to supply one, provided it called for use of its patented 'happiness pills').

Similarly, and very much later, the Canadian Charter of Rights and Freedoms, passed by Parliament in 1982, is all about individual rights and freedoms, guaranteeing that
"Everyone has the following fundamental freedoms:
a) freedom of conscience and religion;
 b) freedom of thought, belief, opinion and expression, including of communication;
c) freedom of peaceful assembly; and
d) freedom of association."

It then assigns a litany of rights, some to citizens and some to everyone: "Every citizen of Canada has the right to vote," "Every citizen of Canada has the right to enter, remain in and leave Canada," and "Everyone has the right to life, liberty and security of the person and the right not to be deprived thereof except in accordance with the principles of fundamental justice, Everyone has the right to be secure against unreasonable search or seizure, and Everyone has the right not to be arbitrarily detained or imprisoned."[32]

Notably, in contrast with the US Bill of Rights, the Canadian Charter of Rights and Freedoms makes no mention of either property rights or the pursuit of happiness.[33]

The language itself, such as "the right not to be..." is indirect and contorted, suggesting an unwillingness to state a moral principle in a secular context and perhaps having doubts about having the authority to do so. But instead of "Everyone has the right not to be arbitrarily detained or imprisoned," the authors could have avoided the ungainly rights language altogether by simply saying that it is illegal to arbitrarily (without cause) detain or imprison

people, or, simply, no one may be arbitrarily detained, etc.;
the Charter is, after all, a legal document.

The qualified and individualistic character of the
rights declared in the increasing number of UN conventions
is clearly expressed in the 1966 International Covenant on
Civil and Political Rights, which actually came into force ten
years later (March 1976). It states in Article 6.1 that "Every
human being has the inherent right to life. This right shall be
protected by law. No one shall be arbitrarily deprived of his
[sic] life." This sounds fine, but objectively it is rather strange
language, reflecting as it does the problem of trying to appear
good while avoiding a 'hard' saying or ethical principle, such
as "You shall not kill." Assigning a person the right to be alive,
that is, stating that they have an "inherent right to life" and
that "no one shall be arbitrarily deprived of his life" would
appear to outlaw war, whether that be a war against 'terrorists'
or drugs or fascism. It would also be reasonable to assume that
a convention that states that "every human being has an
inherent right to life" rules out even the argument for killing
in self defense. But this is the problem presented by moral
commands as opposed to juridical statements which are
always open to, and indeed invite, dispute. Legal dispute,
however, requires a framing context which forbids arbitrary
settlement. There are societies in which disputes are only
settled not by adjudication by a 'neutral' court but when every
party to the dispute agrees to the settlement. This is not a
characteristic of civil law, certainly in North America.[34]

The conditions of a 'right to life' apparently refer only
to individual behaviour governed and limited by established
local or national laws. This interpretation is strengthened by
Article 19 which says that "Everyone shall have the right to
freedom of expression," but the exercise of this right "may ...
be subject to certain restrictions ... for the protection of
national security or of public order (*ordre public*)."[35] No
mention is made of expression being dominated, if not

effectively controlled, by large privately owned media conglomerates that radically limit the possibilities of public expression while exercising their corporate 'right' to freedom of expression of their right-wing, pro-business views in editorials, columns and selection of 'news' to be reported.

The preamble of the UDHR is probably the apex of claims for rights when it speaks of the "inherent dignity" of "all members of the human family" and their "inalienable rights." ("Whereas recognition of the inherent dignity and of the equal and inalienable rights of all members of the human family is the foundation of freedom, justice and peace in the world ...")

The fifth 'whereas' of the preamble assumes a religious orientation for a secular 'universal' declaration when it speaks of "faith in fundamental human rights" and establishes the individualism of rights with reference to "the dignity and worth of the human person." ("Whereas the peoples of the United Nations have in the Charter reaffirmed their faith in fundamental human rights, in the dignity and worth of the human person and in the equal rights of men and women ....") These rights, however, "were held to exist not as legal rights, but as universal moral rights."[36]

There may appear to be a contradiction between natural rights and rights granted, if not created, by the state, but this apparent contradiction can be accommodated by recognizing the distance between philosophical positions and practical behaviour. Natural or ontological rights may well be formally recognized by the society and even the state, while functionally they are treated as a *gift* of the state, a gift that may be constrained or recalled. A copyright is generally granted for a period of 'life plus 50 years', a driver's license may be withdrawn for drunk driving, or a citizen is defined by the state as a 'terrorist' and held as a non-person without rights of any sort.

RIGHTS AND THE STATE

The pragmatic choice (or thoughtless drift) to rely heavily on the discourse of rights to pursue justice for individuals has led to the domination of rights claims over more explicit political and social discourse and programs. It also puts the state at the centre of, or as the focus of, all justice-seeking. Responsibility for justice is assigned to the state, while moral and political responsibilities of the public are over-shadowed or simply ignored, contributing to the neoliberal 'disappearance' of public. Dependency on the state is thereby enhanced.

Such a dependency on the state for implementation of what are referred to as human rights forces the question of the state itself. If one is going to task the state with the implementation of social justice, on the assumption that the state has a positive role to play, then it is important to have a clear understanding of the nature and function of the state, and this must be accompanied by a political program for the state to fulfill.

The advocates of rights, however, actually hold contradictory views of the state, ranging from the conservative libertarian view of the state to the radical anarchist position. As I have pointed out, on the one hand the state is regarded as the enemy (sometimes a necessary enemy) of

personal freedom: rights are for protection *from* the state –
while on the other hand it is regarded as the means to justice:
rights are granted, implemented and enforced *by* the state.
Nevertheless, both accept in practice that the state is
responsible for providing and maintaining the structure and
infrastructure of society, though the latter may be devolved*
to regional and local authorities, or simply privatized. The
state is also responsible for institutional stability and social
welfare, though the meanings of social welfare may differ
widely.

Despite all the talk about democracy being a pre-
requisite of human rights, it is obvious, in practice, that the
demand for recognition of rights is not contingent on any
particular form of government. In recent history rights have
been demanded of dictatorships and fascist governments as
well as communist/socialist countries (Cuba, China etc.). In
other words, both liberals and conservatives direct their
rights demands to the party, or people, in power, regardless
of ideology. The ambiguity of the public toward the state,
and the ambiguity of the state itself, does not appear to enter
into the rights discourse. Any state will do as the recipient of
demands for rights.

Increasingly the 'protection of human rights' has
been associated with bringing about 'regime change' by
violent means in order, at least in theory, to impose
democratic government. While the claim that a state must be
democratic may be good for public relations and selling
political programs in the west, the abstraction of human or
property rights may be of far less value to its citizens than
adequate social welfare and the political stability provided by
an authoritarian state. An anecdote from Iran makes the
point:

---

*Sometimes referred to as the principle of subsidiarity.

"The Shah of Iran was toppled in 1979 and Ayatollah Khomeini flew back from France to take control of the revolution, the *Daheh-ye-Fajr* or '10-day dawn'. A 60-year-old driver said, '*Fajr* means *zajr* [misery]. I took part in demonstrations in 1979 and regret it now. Then we had a welfare system, but we've lost it. The only ones celebrating are the Revolutionary Guards and the militiamen who are paid for it. No one else does'."[37]

Presented as non-partisan and without political program or ideology, human rights advocacy appears as politically safe and non-threatening to a state or an elite. In practice, however, human rights advocacy is often accompanied by insistence on a political program of democratization – whatever that might mean. One need look no further than to the rationalizations offered for the US bombings and invasion of Iraq and Afghanistan. The advocacy of rights at an international level can have serious political consequences when accompanied by, or accompanying, direct military intervention or less direct subversive efforts in sovereign states, regardless of their political make-up.

While not directly addressing human rights advocacy, the following comment on French President Sarkozy's love of crisis management may well apply to much human rights advocacy: "Resolving crises ... substitutes for a longer term political program; urgency has its own meaning and logic, like war, which absolves those involved from providing any meaning of their own for what they do and why."[38]

The absence of political program, or the illusion that there is no political program accompanying human rights advocacy, may be explained by the way in which rights themselves, far from being a matter of means to achieve desired social ends, become the ends themselves. This can lead to profoundly muddled, if not nonsensical and even violent 'rights' demands. As Milan Kundera observed, "The more the fight for human rights gains in popularity, the more it loses any concrete content, becoming a kind of universal stance of everyone towards everything, a kind of energy that turns all human desires into rights."[39]

An extreme example of this tendency is the Genetic Bill of Rights developed by the Council for Responsible Genetics in the US.[40] The first of the rights enumerated is that "All people have the right to preservation of the earth's biological and genetic diversity." This is not a call for a respect for Creation, or a statement that the earth and its diversity have 'rights' of their own, or that we are a part of Creation, but rather an expression of the western capitalist notion that Creation's biological and genetic diversity are to be maintained as 'resources' to meet the demands of capital. Why the Council for Responsible Genetics is calling for this right is not mentioned and they suggest no policies or programs that the state could or should carry out to fulfill this right, though presumably they have thought about them. There is no mention of the effects of global warming, for example, though global warming will certainly have severe effects on biodiversity, and it is a phenomenon that can only be adequately addressed at the state and international level.

The last of the ten rights claimed in the Genetic Bill of Rights shows the extreme to which the rights discourse can carry its adherents. That "all people have the right to have been conceived, gestated, and born without genetic manipulation," suggests that a person who does not yet exist can demand that certain moral, technical and legal conditions be put in place by the government prior to its eventual coming into being. Unfortunately, the Genetic Bill of Rights does not specify how this is to be done, or who has the authority to enforce such a right. Nor does it even suggest that genetic manipulation is immoral or a violation of the dignity and integrity of the organism, at whatever stage of life.

The authors of this Genetic Bill of Rights claim that "the adoption of a right establishes a burden of proof. Those who wish to violate the right must demonstrate a compelling government interest." They do not indicate what this 'compelling government interest' might be, but they apparently accept that there can be a time when the interests of the state can override public interest or public good.

Logically this could mean that the authors of this Genetic Bill of Rights are also implicitly assigning validity to the action of the US Government, in the name of a 'compelling government interest', in its non-judicial treatmended of those it chooses to identify as terrorists – an action carried out in the name of defending the USA.

It should be obvious, as the Indigenous of Mexico point out, that there is little point in making demands on the state for rights when it is the state itself that is the violator of human and property rights, either directly, by proxy, or simply negligence, that is, by overlooking the activities of armed militias acting for landowners, mining companies and drug cartels or the illegal activities of its own military and police.

The USA passed its Bill of Rights in 1791 as the first ten amendments to its constitution, as I have mentioned. Congress, having given legitimacy to the state and defined its jurisdiction in the Constitution itself, then saw fit to lay down explicit limitations on the authority of that state. That has not, however, ensured the practice of social, economic, political or legal justice, since the Bill of Rights is all about limiting the powers of the state over individuals within its jurisdiction, not establishing the criteria for positive economic or social justice in the country. These are negative rights – things the state is not supposed to do or interfere with.

Canada got along without a Charter of Rights and Freedoms until quite recently, with arguably more social justice than is to be found in the USA, and the United Kingdom has neither a written constitution nor a declaration of rights.

Even if rights are granted and/or recognized, they still have to be given substance: there is no inherent nutrition, for example, in the 'right to food'. It is a political demand without a program for both the government and for those calling for the right, even if it is considered incumbent on the grantor of the right (the state) to provide real food to real people. This is, of course, the reason some activists have adopted the language of the right to food, hoping it can be used to force the state to take responsibility for feeding the people – or at least not make it impossible for people to feed themselves.

Even if the right to food is granted, what kind of food would be available or delivered as a result? Would it be healthy, ecologically produced food or would it simply be more of the industrial food that is already supplied by the giant corporations currently dominating the food system? Given the intimate relationship between the corporate food sector and the state, the food that might be made available could simply increase overall dependency on the corporate industrial food system.

Rather than calling on the state to establish a right to food, a growing number of people are now organizing local food systems to meet the needs of their communities. They are also organizing seed saving and doing it, and while acknowledging that not everyone is in a position to save seeds or supply food, they recognize a public responsibility to create a political climate in which seed saving and food sovereignty are understood to be public goods and encouraged by the state as a matter of policy. The right to food and the right to save seeds is simply not enough.

A fine example of community leadership in meeting the food needs of its people can be found in India, which has a national Public Distribution System that is supposed to ensure that no one goes hungry. In Andhra Pradesh, the Deccan Development Society (DDS) decided to make this more of a local reality than just a national policy. It persuaded the national government to give it the money that would otherwise have been spent on the Public Distribution System in the area in which DDS works. DDS then got villagers to select local committees of woman to identify the individuals and families most in need of food. Instead of the food then coming from national warehouses, DDS purchases the food required by each village from local farmers. The 'right to food' is thus fulfilled by the villages from local farmers, utilizing the funds coming from the national government out of general tax revenues. The food is grown from seeds selected and saved by the farmers or from seeds supplied by the village seed keeper for dryland crops such as sorghum and millet, rather than alien crops such as wheat or maize.

PROPERTY RIGHTS:
HUMAN AND CORPORATE

The conflation – or confusion – of human rights and property rights can be attributed, in European and North
American culture and society, to the claim that property is
essential to or an expression of human identity and dignity
– or at least the identity and dignity of some humans, usually
the propertied class. Therefore property rights are human
rights.

Responsibility for both the claims and the confusion
is generally attributed to the English philosopher John Locke
(1632-1704), who wrote that,

"Though the Earth, and all inferior Creatures be
common to all Men, yet every Man has property in his
own Person. This no Body has any Right to but
himself. The Labour of his Body and the Work of his
Hands ... are properly his. Whatsoever then he re-
moves out of the State that Nature hath provided, and
left it in, he hath mixed his Labour with, and joined it
to something that is his own, and thereby makes it his
Property."[41]

Locke added that there must be "enough, and as good left in common for others" and that no person take from the commons more than he can use.

Following Locke, property rights came to be regarded by the European project of Enlightenment and the capitalist systems that flowed from it as an essential attribute of being human, an expression of a person's being human.[42]

Of course, we must recognize that Locke was living and writing in a pre-industrial age. What 'Man' could "remove out of the State of Nature" was extremely limited, unless aided and abetted by serfs, slaves, or imperial armies. 'Man' was, at that time, quite incapable of depleting fish stocks or destroying entire forests, though there is a school of thought that attributes the decline and fall of the Mayan empire – and perhaps the Roman empire and others – to the destruction of the environment that sustained them. Nevertheless, "The *Labour* of his Body and the *Work* of his Hands" – which would have appeared to have reasonable limits in John Locke's day – became highly expansionary and destructive with industrialization and the rise of capitalism with its essential ethic of growth. Individual 'rights' and the 'rights' of capital became inseparable social forces as the rights of property.

A greater leap came with the endowment of a corporation with the status of a person before the law. The common law recognition of corporations as persons, albeit artificial, is generally traced back to Wm. Blackstone in the mid-18th century when he wrote in his Commentaries on the Laws of England:

"Persons also are divided by the law into either natural persons, or artificial. Natural persons are such as the God of nature formed us: artificial are such as created and devised by human laws for the purposes of society and government; which are called corporations or bodies politic."[43]

Historically, the corporation appeared earlier as Crown appointed trading companies, such as the East India Company, chartered in 1600, or the Hudson's Bay Company, chartered in 1670 to trade in furs in what is today northern and western Canada. These corporations, and others, were assigned the powers of the Crown in the territories in which they traded, anywhere in the world, inclouding the power to raise their own armies and organize civil administration. However, they were still expected to serve the interests of the Crown and empire and did not have license to act in their own interests against those of their sponsor as privateers. They were not granted sovereignty.

Since the latter years of the 19th century, corporations, in their legal guise of artificial person and citizen, have increasingly asserted their sovereign, if not natural, rights in libertarian fashion against and over the state. Assuming the prerogatives of royalty, the corporation uses the state as its proxy, rewarding well the agents of the state (civil servants and others) that faithfully execute the corporate will. Rights, both human and property, are assumed by the corporate *persona* and given, by the corporation, priority over the rights of natural persons. The health of a society, then, is measured by its rate of economic growth and the rise in share prices on the stock market rather than in terms of the well-being of its citizens. Such rights that may be granted to natural persons, such as you and me, by the state become highly contingent exemptions to the broader rights (and powers) of the corporations.

Any discussion of rights, and any assumption of the universality of human rights, must consider the implications of granting rights to entities which also have legally limited liability. This applies to both the legal body of the corporation and its board of directors and the shareholders. In other words, there is no personal liability for what the corporation does or does not do. However, as Jeffrey Kaplan points out, "As late as 1840, US state legislators closely supervised the operation of corporations, allowing them to be created only for very specific public benefits, such as the building of a highway or a canal. Corporations were subject to a variety of limitations: a finite period of existence, limits to the amount of property they could own, and prohibitions against one corporation owning another."[44]

These limitations gradually gave way before the rise of corporate power in the US, and by the 1860s "most states had granted owners limited liability, waiving virtually all personal accountability for an institution's cumulative actions." Then in 1886, the United States Supreme Court, in *Santa Clara County v. Southern Pacific Railroad*, extended the logic of the corporation as an artificial entity to grant it the identity of a natural person with natural rights, thereby opening the door to corporate claims to rights under the US Bill of Rights.[45]

The elaboration and extension of the rights and power of corporations in the neo-liberal era, aided and abetted by the neo-liberal demands for deregulation and free trade, has stood Blackstone on his head. The artificial person created by law for the purposes of society and government takes command of law and government and the privileges of the corporation take precedence over the needs and desires of natural persons and their societies.*[46]

In fact, there are powerful examples of the demands of corporations for their rights going directly against justice, equity and the public good, such as the demands of Big Pharma for patent and copyright 'protection' of their drugs,

---

* "To simplify greatly, the general view [of the 19th century Left, Marx in particular] is that 'property rights' as they are commonly known are at most an artificial construct, masking the force and oppression of the powerful few and duping the rest of us into going along with their hegemonic pretensions."[45]

Monsanto's enforcement of its patents on its seeds, the expansive copyright claims of Big Media or Coca-Cola's claim of its right to water. Then there is the most egregious example of the exploitation of rights for corporate advertising of products such as tobacco and other drugs in the name of freedom of expression.

This corporate supremacy has found its extreme expression in the various neoliberal trade regimes, such as the North American Free Trade Agreement and a wide variety of bi-lateral 'free trade' agreements in which states agree to assign rights to corporations and their investors (owners) that give them a certain degree of sovereignty over the states they wish to operate or invest in. In the case of the North American Free Trade Agreement (NAFTA, effective since 1994), Article 1102: National Treatment, says that:

"1. Each Party [i.e. signatory national state] "shall accord to investors of another Party treatment no less favorable than that it accords, in like circumstances, to its own investors with respect to the establishment, acquisition, expansion, management, conduct, operation, and sale or other disposition of investments.

"2. Each Party shall accord to investments of investors of another Party treatment no less favorable than that it accords, in like circumstances, to investments of its own investors ...

"3. The treatment accorded by a Party under paragraphs 1 and 2 means, with respect to a state or province, treatment no less favorable than the most favorable treatment accorded, in like circumstances, by that state or province to investors, and to investments of investors, of the Party of which it forms a part."

In other words, the rights ceded to the corporations and their investors by sovereign states in the trade agreements give them power over the states, while requiring the states to enforce the rights they have granted to the corporations, referred to as National Treatment. Disputes are settled by panels appointed by the parties to the agreements not in terms of justice, but in terms of the legal agreement (contract) made by the parties.

A good example of the intent of NAFTA to protect capital, however accumulated, is the situation of Abitibi-Bowater in Newfoundland. In 1905 the government of Newfoundland (a colony of Britain from 1707 to 1907 which became a Province of Canada in 1949) made an agreement with the company that is now Abitibi Bowater Inc. to lease the company extensive timber and water rights in return for building and operating a paper mill on the site, now the town of Grand Falls-Windsor. In December, 2008, the company announced that it planned to close the mill. With that, the Premier of Newfoundland announced that the Province would expropriate the company's timber and water rights and physical hydroelectric and mill assets, compensating the company for these facilities at a rate deemed fair by the Province. The Province claims the expropriation is fair because the 1905 lease agreement was explicit that the water and timber rights were dependent on the company operating a mill in the province. The company says it will challenge the expropriation under NAFTA since the company is now a US entity.

Another example arose from the intention of the Province of Québec to ban lawn (non-industrial, cosmetic) pesticides containing 2,4-D. Dow AgroSciences, a US company, is claiming $2 million in compensation under NAFTA for lost business if the Québec Government goes ahead with the ban. Dow said the Québec ban was not driven by science but by "political, social or cultural considerations." Federal Trade Minister Stockwell Day said "The NAFTA preserves the state's ability to regulate in the public interest, including public health and environmental issues related to pesticides." To which Dow countered, "we filed this notice to protect our rights under NAFTA."[47] In its lawsuit, which is to go to a three-member NAFTA arbitration panel, Dow accuses Canada of breaching its obligations under Chapter 11 of NAFTA and seeks damages covering loss of sales, profits, goodwill, investment and other costs related to the products.[48]

In this age of corporate impersonation – corporations pretending on both legal and moral grounds to be persons and claiming all the rights of persons for purposes of enhancing their dominance and profits – the conflation of *human* and *property* rights must be contested.[49] It is reasonable, in the context of western law for corporations to hold well-defined material property rights. It is not reasonable under any regime for a corporation to be able to claim 'human' rights for itself.

PROPERTY RIGHTS AND THE
RIGHT OF PROPERTY

A property right, or 'right in property' as it is sometimes
referred to, might playfully be characterized as *the right of
property* to be owned, and owned exclusively. That is, we
might consider it the inherent right of property, as such, to
exclude any or all persons from access to or enjoyment of
it[self]. Historically, of course, this applied to land and
moveable material property (jewels, food commodities)[50] but
more recently it has come to be applied to immaterial loca-
tionless property, referred to as 'intellectual' property (music,
writing, and much more, to be discussed later). Aspects of the
stock market, such as 'futures' and 'derivatives' are even more
immaterial, and might be described as fictional property that
can be bought and sold, but which are really only apparitions
that appear in the terms of contracts and promises. This
apparitional character became painfully obvious with the
collapse of the markets, and the stock markets in particular,

in 2008-2009. The value of this fictional property simply evaporated.

There is also a category of contentious property rights known as mineral or sub-soil rights which refer to the privilege, granted by the state to a person or corporation, to gain access to and claim ownership over, and right to exploit, what lies underground, such as oil, gold or potash, regardless of who owns the visible property or surface rights. Water, as a commodity, is even more contentious since in most instances it does not stand still. Even an aquifer is in constant motion and a well on one property may draw water from beneath another property that holds rights to water in the same aquifer. There are also obvious conflicts between states over the rights to the water in a river that crosses juris-dictional boundaries. Of course, all such conflicts arise be-cause the minerals, water and elements are considered as, and given the legal status of, ownable commodities in the first place. Needless to say, the idea that Creation and its elements can be owned – by anybody – is not universally accepted. (I, for one, cannot conceive of 'owning' water or of water being able to be owned by anybody.)

In western legal tradition, the rights to property can be held by both natural and artificial (corporate) persons. Going further, rights themselves become property, that is, tradable commodities (as do patents and copyrights) with some contemporary corporations' assets consisting solely of a patent portfolio. Rights as property then creates a category of owners referred to, particularly in regard to copyright, as 'rights holders'. In contemporary discussion and legislation concerning copyright, this new category of rights-holders, specifically in the form of the corporate media-entertainment industry, is the power broker/property-owner between crea-tors – authors, musicians and artists – and the public. (I will discuss copyright and other forms of IP later.)

There is a Western legal position that holds property to be a 'bundle of rights', one of which may or may not be that of exclusion from the use or enjoyment of the property. Urban real estate ownership, for example, carries with it a variety of encumbrances and responsibilities, privileges and liabilities, evident in zoning regulations, noise bylaws and taxes for various purposes, indicating that rights can be limited as well as granted by the state. In the USA, however, there is a strong ideological movement that refers to any limitations imposed by the state on private property as 'takings', including 'taking' land, with compensation, under the right of eminent domain, for public purposes such as roads and parks. This is a rare example of a public right taking precedence over individual property rights.

Human rights and property rights become even more scrambled when human rights are interpreted as exclusionary rights. That is, they are treated as the right of a person to exclude (and be protected from) violation and exploitation.

The campaign against violence against women has been a kind of positivist exclusion, both individual and collective. But again, it has not been a campaign for the individual right to be free of the threat and exercise of domination and violence, but for a change in the social attitude towards women that would greatly reduce violence inflicted on women. In contrast, a rights-based approach finds expression in language such as "violence against women and girls is not only a violation of fundamental rights, it destroys the social fabric of communities". Apparently, according to this language, violence against women is not bad because women are hurt, maimed, degraded and shamed, but because it is a violation of rights. Another sentence on the same page of the Canadian Council for International Cooperation's 10-point Agenda says "migrant workers ... are vulnerable to exploitation and rights violations." It is not obvious why the violation of rights has to be continually inserted in otherwise meaningful language.

A collective manifestation of this exclusionary right is the gated community, wherein individuals collectively, as well as individually in their houses, assert their right to exclude the public (regarded as intruders) from their property/persons. This conflation of human and property right finds its extreme expression in the US Bill of Rights which says that no person "shall be ... deprived of life, liberty or property, without due process of law". The recurring practice of slavery, wherein the person quite literally becomes property, simultaneously denies the slave of liberty while ensuring that the slave's owner is not deprived of 'enjoyment' of his property. Presumably this is outlawed under this provision of the Bill of Rights.

Unfortunately, the distance between overt slavery and the wage slaves – cheap labour – that produce and service an increasing proportion of the property of the Western wealthy and comparatively wealthy is not as great as may first appear.

Rights are never as absolute as their 'owners' might like to think – for which the lawyers handling the lawsuits over who owns what are grateful.

RIGHT TO FOOD
AND THE EMPTY BOWL

We took up commercial farming in Nova Scotia in 1971. Two years later the Arab states imposed an oil embargo and this led to a stock market crash in 1973-4. Most of our neighbour-friends were back-to-the-land hippie types. We were all growing most of our own food. The oil crisis and stock market crash had little effect on us – we were too young to be thinking about our pension funds and had little 'cash flow'. But we did talk about what the city folks might do when faced with a serious food shortage. Would they come to us begging for food? Would they come claiming their right to our food? Or would they come with guns to steal our food? What would we do? We could not possibly feed a crowd from New Glasgow, much less a mob from Halifax. Should we arm ourselves? It was interesting to see how at least some of our friends realized, in this discourse, the ultimate impossibility of isolation from society and started to work for social justice in a variety of ways to ward off the nightmare of folks with guns raiding their gardens and freezers. Fortunately the mob never arrived.

The principal international 'norm' on the Right to Food is contained within Article 11 of the International Convention on Economic, Social, and Cultural Rights, which was adopted in December 1966, entered into force in January, 1976, and has been binding on Canada since 1976. The Preamble of the Convention states "that these rights derive from the inherent dignity of the human person," thus placing these rights firmly within the culture of western individualism.

The Convention does not explain how rights derive from dignity, but uses it as a starting point. If rights are assumed to be universal, their starting point cannot be a particular religious or cultural belief. Natural law presents similar problems. Dignity, however, is apparently of some substance and neutral.

Article 11 of the Convention describes the ingredients in the stew:

1. The States Parties to the present Covenant recognize the right of everyone to an adequate standard of living for himself and his family, including adequate food, clothing and housing, and to the continuous improvement of living conditions ...

2. The States Parties to the present Covenant, recognizing the fundamental right of everyone to be free from hunger, shall take, individually and through international co-operation, the measures, including specific programmes, which are needed:

(a) To improve methods of production, conservation and distribution of food by making full use of technical and scientific knowledge, by disseminating knowledge of the principles of nutrition and by developing or reforming agrarian systems in such a way as to achieve the most efficient development and utilization of natural resources;

(b) Taking into account the problems of both food-importing and food-exporting countries, to ensure an equitable distribution of world food supplies in relation to need.

The language of this covenant is a fairly extreme expression of the very singular culture of the Enlightenment and the industrial revolution, with its assumption of universality, progress and development through science and technology, as in: "continuous improvement in living conditions ... improve methods of production ... making full use of technical and scientific knowledge ... principles of nutrition ... most efficient development and utilization of natural resources." The idea of the right to food is thus intimately bound within a particular culture that stresses legal and contractual relations, not social relations and responsibility, and technological rather than social means of implementing it.

The particularity of this culture extends to what it assumes to be the proper, if not only, way to produce the food that would be required to fulfill the obligation of the right to food. In explicitly citing "methods of production" that "make full use of technical and scientific knowledge," other forms of agriculture and the experience, skills and knowledge of traditional food providers are excluded as being neither technical nor scientific. In their place, if we consider the activities and policies of the Food and Agriculture Organization of the UN until very recently, is the "technical and scientific knowledge" on which the western model of industrial agriculture is based, including synthetic fertilizers, agrotoxins (agricultural chemicals), monoculture cropping and more recently, genetic engineering.

A case study of the Right to Food in Canada, carried out for the Food and Agriculture Organization of the UN (FAO) by Graham Riches, states that,

"The human right to adequate food is a legal right which addresses head-on the moral, political and social issues relating to food poverty and food insecurity in Canada at the present time ... Food insecurity for many Canadians raises issues of human rights and distributive justice culminating in state action and policies or programs implemented through legislation."[51]

Two years previously, the FAO's Special Rapporteur on the Right to Food, Jean Ziegler, had reported that while the United Nations agencies "emphasize social justice and human rights," the World Bank and International Monetary Fund, along with the Government of the United States and the World Trade Organization, oppose the right to food by emphasizing trade liberalization (including food commodities), deregulation, privatization, and abolition of regulations that impede market entry or restrict competition policies which in many cases produce greater inequalities.[52] In 2007-08 the consequences of these policies went far beyond 'inequalities' to severe malnutrition, sickness and starvation, brought on, in part, by the systematic destruction of local food systems virtually dictated by the World Bank and the profiteering escalation of commodity prices.

In other words, the concept of the Right to Food is something less than a clarion call for social justice. In fact, it is fair to say that while the Right to Food may be a globally popular term, it is little more than a morally upright principle without a cost to those in command of food production and distribution. It says nothing about how food is to be produced, where food is to come from, or who is to get it at what price.

Nor is there any indication of who is obliged to ensure that everyone gets enough to eat; customary use of the term 'rights' would indicate that it is a government responsibility, though despite Riches' assertion that it culminates in

state action, it is not justiciable, that is, there is no legal
authority to enforce it. Even when accepted on principle, it
remains just a principle and nothing more. The best the UN
Commission on Human Rights can do was expressed in a
resolution on the right to food (introduced by Cuba and
passed by a vote of 52 for, 1 against: the USA) in 2005 that
"Encourages all States to take steps with a view to achieving
progressively the full realization of the right to food ... "[53]

In his 2007 Report to the UN General Assembly, the
Special Rapporteur on the Right to Food could, once again,
only make a moral appeal, relying on the word 'should' in the
absence of any legal authority for enforcement of his con-
clusions and recommendations, saying that "Hunger is not
inevitable" and that "all States should take immediate action
to realize the human right to food of all their people." The
rigidity and juridical orientation of the rights language pro-
duces the unfortunately sterile conclusion that "leaving
people to suffer from hunger, famine and starvation is a violation of human rights"[54] – rather than immoral or unethical
or even criminal.

To define an issue as a right and not a moral issue and
to channel it to the state also obscures the fact that it is
capitalism, in the form of the dominant corporate sector,
which is actually defining where food comes from, under
what conditions, and who gets it at what price. If the state
actually intended to accept and implement the human right
to food, it would have to limit corporate control of and profit
from the food system. The current globalized industrial
production of food would also have to undergo a
transformation into a decentralized ecologically sound
diversity of methods, as noted in 2008 by the current UN
Special Rapporteur:

"... it is the considered view of the Special Rapporteur,
who shares the analysis of the Committee on

Economic, Social and Cultural Rights on this issue [referring to the failure by States to regulate activities of individuals or groups so as to prevent them from violating the right to food of others as an instance of the violation of the right to food] that this implies an obligation of all States to effectively protect the right to food by regulating the activities of companies at all levels of the system of production and distribution of food."[55]

A direct moral appeal to the public for the construction of an equitable and ecological food system might, actually, be more politically effective and morally satisfying – though much harder – than appealing to governments for the right to food. Such a direct, public approach, or attitude, is captured by the term 'food sovereignty' which has rapidly gained popular usage around the world. Urban community gardens are a highly practical expression of this moral initiative, and can be found from Canada to Cuba. An even more direct assertion of food sovereignty is the occupation of idle or underused farm lands by the 'landless', as in Brazil, accompanied by the demand that the state recognize their 'title' in the land. Similarly, urban homeless around the world have long engaged in 'squatting' in vacant residential and industrial buildings, buildings often slated for demolition to make way for the 'rights' of the rich.

Food sovereignty was the subject of a gathering of some 600-700 people from around the world in Nyéléni, Mali, West Africa, in February, 2007. The following is the introduction to the Synthesis Report of the gathering:

"Nyéléni was the inspiration for the name of our Forum for Food Sovereignty in Sélingué, Mali. Nyéléni was a legendary Malian peasant woman who farmed and fed her people well – she embodied food sovereignty through hard work, innovation and caring for her people. We, peasant farmers, pastoralists, fisherfolk, indigenous peoples, migrant workers, women and young people, who gathered at Nyéléni 2007 are food providers who are ready, able and willing to feed all the world's peoples. Our heritage as providers of food is critical to the future of humanity. This is especially so in the case of women and indigenous peoples who are historical creators of knowledge about food, agriculture and traditional aquaculture. But this heritage and our capacity to produce healthy, good and abundant food are being threatened and undermined by neo-liberalism and global capitalism.

We debated food sovereignty issues in order to: a) deepen collective understanding; b) strengthen dialogue among and between sectors and interest groups; and c) formulate joint strategies and an action agenda. Our debates gave food providers as well as environmentalists, consumers and urban movements the strength and power to fight for food sovereignty in Mali, the rest of Africa and worldwide.

Through our alliances, we can join together to preserve, recover and build on our knowledge in order to strengthen the essential capacity that leads to sustaining localised food systems. In realizing food sovereignty, we will also ensure the survival of our cultures, our peoples and of the Earth."[56]

The Canadian Indigenous Food Sovereignty Working Group has identified several key principles of Indigenous food sovereignty, the first being "Sacredness – Food is a gift from the Creator; we have a sacred responsibility to nurture healthy, interdependent relationships with the land, plants and animals that provide us with our food."[57]

Among Indigenous peoples worldwide can be found clusters and crowds of people seeking to regain their language and traditional foodways, knowing that if they do not, their

very identity will disappear. They do not speak of their right
to do so. They speak, instead, of their responsibilities to care
for each other and Creation, through which they, along with
other species, receive the gift of food.

The pursuit of rights, on the other hand, is an attempt
to work within a highly individualistic secular context in
which the moral imperatives of the web of relationships that
constitute a society are unrecognized. Underlying every claim
for rights is a highly problematic attitude concerning what is
due to a person. The claim of a right to food is an expression of
an alienated attitude of entitlement rather than gratitude.
Gratitude for the abundance of Creation is certainly more
intimate than a claim of entitlement and carries with it a sense
of responsibility.

FARMERS' RIGHTS
AND PLANT BREEDERS' RIGHTS

While visiting a small village in Andra Pradesh, India, I was told by the village seed keeper, a dalit *(Untouchable) woman, that one year the wealthy farmer in the village experienced total crop failure. Left with none of his own seeds for planting in the next season, he had to turn to the* dalit *village seed keeper for seeds, thus rupturing the rigid caste structure of the village and opening the way to new social relations.*

In spite of being used quite widely by a variety of very diverse elements, from peasant farmers and their militant organizations to UN agencies and seed companies such as Monsanto, the term 'farmers' rights' is certainly one of the most pernicious constructs of the rights language. What are mistakenly referred to as farmers' rights are essentially the collective prerogative of a class of people (farmers and gardeners) to practice and participate in the social custom of selecting, saving, swapping and replanting seeds from year to year. These activities can be described as the 'custodial responsibilities' of farmers, gardeners and subsistence peoples for seeds and the knowledge about them. These practices and responsibilities are not granted by any authority, though they may be honoured by a rural community or village in recognition of their importance.

The observance of, not rights to, customary /traditional practices and knowledge – from seed saving to land management – is a matter of social, cultural and physical survival, not an individual business practice or a demand for legal status. Treating seeds as a commodity, and referring to the traditional practices of saving, swapping and replanting seed as a 'right', is a disrespectful dismissal of an essential and customarily sacred element in the lives of millions of people around the world today and throughout history.

Once seeds are defined as property, the issue becomes not how seeds are cared for but whose property they are. Since the middle of the 20th century, seeds have increasingly become the commercial property of corporations,[58] which use the mechanisms of hybridization, certification, genetic engineering, patents and contract production to exercise their *appropriated* 'ownership rights' over seed.* The customary agricultural practice of seed saving then becomes an exception to, or exemption from, the rule of capital.**

The powerful, in the form of state, class or corporation, can and do *assume* privileges for themselves. They may also *grant* privileges, in the form of rights, to less powerful supplicants. Thus corporations now assume for themselves Plant Breeders' Rights—with approval and legitimation by the state – while they in turn would grant farmers the *privilege* – as 'farmers' right' – of saving their own seeds for a season. It is assumed, in this scenario, that plant breeding is a professional activity carried out in the formal sector of corporations, universities and public agricultural research

---

* The first Plant Patent Act was only passed in the USA in 1930.

** This 'enclosure' of the seed harks back to the enclosure of the village commons by the feudal lords of England in the 18th and 19th centuries.

institutions, while farmers, languishing in the informal sector, are apt to be deemed incapable of 'scientific' plant breeding, if only because of the cost. Under capitalism, they are tolerated (or even required as a source of 'genetic resources') but not valued.

In this context, plant breeders set themselves up as members of a professional scientific society with responsibility for defining their own credentials, standards and regulation. In so doing they appropriate the function of traditional farmers as plant breeders as well as seed savers and define custody and breeding of plants and crops as their professional prerogative (right) recognized by the state. Recognition of Plant Breeders' Rights also inhibits the development of collaborative farmer-breeder relationships by limiting access to and work with 'protected' varieties and proprietary germplasm by requiring licensing arrangements with the institutional and corporate rights holders. Fortunately, there are still some plant breeders employed in universities and government departments who regard themselves as working in the public sector for the good of farmers and the public.[59]

Once formal seed breeders (and their employers) had captured plant breeding and seed propagation, they started to claim that it was their right to profit by such commercial enterprise. Then the traditional functions and practices of farmers were regarded as a threat and the traditional practice of seed saving was redefined as a privilege – a privilege granted by commercial seed 'owners' with state backing. The only remaining rights for the farmer are 'users rights', that is, the 'right' to plant, cultivate, harvest and sell the crop produced by the seed that essentially remains the property of its corporate owner. The farmer, then, effectively only *rents* the seed for a season.

Similarly, users' rights are now appearing in the language of the media conglomerates with reference to the 'rights' of the purchaser of a book or record to read or listen to the purchase they have made. Big Media now wants, in effect, to limit users' rights by asserting perpetual ownership with the ability to collect royalties on every 're-use' of what has already been purchased.

The assertion of Farmers' Rights is intended to create the legal space for farmers to maintain these traditional practices in the face of efforts, by both states and corporations, to enclose this space and occupy it with hybrids, patented varieties and corporate agents while outlawing the traditional practices. Thus Farmers' Rights are functionally a reactive claim for an exception to the capitalist laws of private property.

The idea of Farmers' Rights[*][60] arose as a defence against the increasing dominance of Plant Breeders' Rights (PBR) only after the establishment in 1961 of the International Union for the Protection of New Plant Varieties (UPOV)[**][61] that created the legal curiosity of Plant Breeders'

---

[*] "The subject matter of farmers' rights are first and foremost traditional crop varieties, their wild and weedy relatives and the related knowledge and innovations of their custodians."[56]

[**] "The idea of farmers' rights emerged from the debate on intellectual property rights (IPRs) on plant genetic resources (PGRs) in the early 1980s, as voiced in international negotiations. At that time, the signatories to the International Undertaking on Plant Genetic Resources of the United Nations Food and Agriculture Organization (FAO) discussed how they could attract the signatures of more countries, as this was [considered] pivotal to realizing the objectives of conserving these resources and making them available. Many Northern countries set the recognition of plant breeders' rights (PBRs) as a precondition for joining the International Undertaking. However, many developing countries were opposed to it, seeing such rights as against the objectives of the Undertaking and, in addition, unfair, since plant breeders add only the final few links to the hard work and innovations that farmers, particularly in developing countries, have carried out for hundreds and thousands of years. The solution to this conflict was that PBRs were

(continued...)

Rights. As late as 1983 there was still no documented mention of farmers' rights. While breeders' rights are now recognized by national legislation in many countries, so-called farmers' rights have not been given legal recognition.[62] The UPOV Convention of 1961 established criteria for plant varieties (distinct, uniform, stable and novel) that gave plant breeders rights over (ownership of) the commercial propagation of their 'protected' varieties, but UPOV 61 does not restrict farmers from saving seeds or breeders from doing further breeding with the protected varieties.[63] In 1991, however, UPOV was tightened up and the exceptions to Plant Breeders' Rights in the 1961 agreement were curtailed. Currently, some countries have signed on to UPOV 91, including the USA, while others, including Canada, have not, although the corporate seed industry lobbies relentlessly to get the government to sign on to it. New signers have no choice: they have to sign on to UPOV 91.*

**(...continued)
recognised along with farmers' rights by the FAO Conference in 1989."[57]

* In August, 2009, the journal *Scientific American* published an editorial condemning corporate control over independent seed research, saying, "Unfortunately, it is impossible to verify that genetically modified crops perform as advertised. That is because agritech companies have given themselves veto power over the work of independent researchers. To purchase genetically modified seeds, a customer must sign an agreement that limits what can be done with them. [If you have installed software recently, you will recognize the concept of the end-user agreement.] Agreements are considered necessary to protect a company's intellectual property, and they justifiably preclude the replication of the genetic enhancements that make the seeds unique. But agritech companies such as Monsanto, Pioneer and Syngenta go further. For a decade their user agreements have explicitly forbidden the use of the seeds for any independent research. Under the threat of litigation, scientists cannot test a seed to explore the different conditions under which it thrives or fails. They cannot compare seeds from one company against those from

(continued...)

In using, and in allowing the use of, the term Plant Breeders' Rights, farmers are, in effect, recognizing the authority and legitimacy of those who would deny them one of their major traditional customs, a foundation stone of their viability, and a necessity for public food sovereignty.

It is a stunningly opportunistic contradiction that those who claim formal ownership of seeds (and now 'genetics') and lobby for complete privatization of the seed sector also demand state protection of what they claim as their monopoly ('natural') rights, the rights of plant breeders being granted by the state and 'protected' by state legal systems and international treaties. Like all treaties, these are a form of contract law to protect the interests of the contracting parties, not the public as a whole, thus radically changing the character of seed and plant replication and use from public good to private profit.

Without the state there would be no Plant Breeders' Rights, no copyright and no patents. Farmers who save, select and use their own seed, on the other hand, neither have nor require such state 'protection' to go about their work, though they now have to face the threat and experience of having their own seed stocks contaminated by corporate-owned genetically engineered seeds, the corporate right to produce and sell such seed now being authorized by the state. This leaves the farmer having to appeal to the same state for protection from the activities of a corporation backed by the state. Regine Andersen, who provides a most careful and critical discussion of the development and use of farmers' rights, concludes that "Farmers' rights represent a strategic

---

*(...continued)

another company. And perhaps most important, they cannot examine whether the genetically modified crops lead to unintended environmental side effects. Research on genetically modified seeds is still published, of course. But only studies that the seed companies have approved ever see the light of a peer-reviewed journal."

instrument to create legal space within the legislative contexts in the various countries – to ensure that farmers' practices of maintaining agro-biodiversity can continue."[64] This argument is similar to that used by Latin Americans regarding human rights, as discussed earlier.

While in theory legal rights are intended to protect the interests and practices of rights holders, in the case of farmers' rights farmers are explicitly alienated from their customary practices as their rights "are vested in the International Community, as trustee for present and future generations of farmers."[65]

The seed production protected by Plant Breeders' Rights is an integral part of industrial agricultural production. The traditional, and once universal, practice and culture of seed saving and plant breeding, on the other hand, can only be fully exercised within the context of a people whose identity and existence is recognized and respected – including subsistence farmers. Recognition of a people, tribe, clan etc. also requires recognition of and respect for the conditions which make its collective life possible, including land, language and traditional wild and culturally important foodways and the knowledge, passed on from generation to generation, that underlies all these practices.

A clear expression of traditional 'seed sovereignty' – the holding and taking responsibility for the seeds required for a self-sustaining food economy – is a Declaration of Seed Sovereignty by the New Mexico Acequia [irrigators] Association.[66] Making no mention of rights, it is simply a bold statement of intention concerning seeds:

> 21. Be it resolved by the traditional farmers of Indo-Hispano and Native American ancestry of current-day northern New Mexico [that we] collectively and intentionally seek to continue the seed-saving traditions of our ancestors and maintain the

landraces that are indigenous to the region of northern New Mexico.

22. Be it further resolved that we seek to engage youth in the continuation of the traditions of growing traditional foods, sharing scarce water resources, sharing seeds, and celebrating our harvests.

23. Be it further resolved that we reject the validity of corporations' ownership claims to crops and wild plants that belong to our cultural history and identity.

24. Be it further resolved that we believe corporate ownership claims of landrace crop genomes and patent law represent a legal framework for the justification of the possession and destruction of stolen cultural property.

25. Be it further resolved that we object to the seed industry's refusal to label seeds or products containing GE technology and ingredients and demand all genetically modified seeds and foods containing GE ingredients in the State of New Mexico to be labeled as such.

26. Be it further resolved that we consider genetic modification and the potential contamination of our landraces by GE technology a continuation of genocide upon indigenous people and as malicious and sacrilegious acts toward our ancestry, culture, and future generations.

30. Be it further resolved that the undersigned traditional farmers representing various acequia, Pueblo, tribal, and surrounding communities will create, support, and collaborate toward projects and programs focused on revitalization of food traditions, agriculture, and seed saving and sharing.

Following the making of this declaration, the New Mexico state legislature passed a motion "recognizing the significance of indigenous agricultural practice and native seeds to New Mexico's cultural heritage and food security."[67]

To illustrate the importance of language and the choice of particular words, here is an analogous statement of another Indigenous group three years earlier followed by my rephrasing of it:

"We hold sovereign rights over our knowledge, biological diversity and its components. An international regime must expressly affirm the right of indigenous peoples to restrict and or exclude access to their knowledge ... Indigenous peoples are custodians of their Indigenous Knowledge and have the exclusive right to control and manage their knowledge."[68]

In my rewording of this, I have taken back the power and authority given by the language of rights to external authority:

We claim sovereign jurisdiction over our knowledge and biological diversity. Indigenous peoples are custodians of their Indigenous Knowledge and have exclusive responsibility for restricting or excluding access to their knowledge. An international regime must expressly affirm the authority of indigenous peoples to control and manage their knowledge.

If the concept and application of farmers' rights remains elusive, perhaps this is because farmers' rights is an unworkable – and to many, literally unthinkable – idea or concept because it is an alien cultural construct.[*][69] What we

---

* Here I must acknowledge the substantial, ongoing efforts to give real meaning to the concept of farmers' rights through the International Treaty on Plant Genetic Resources for Food and Agriculture. "The realization of Farmers' Rights is a cornerstone in the implementation of the Treaty as it is a precondition for the conservation and sustainable use of these vital resources in situ as well as on-farm. The Treaty

(continued...)

need is state action to curb the predatory practices of the privatizers, the PBR and patent pushers, in the interests of the public good, present and future. It is ownership of the seed (and its 'genetics') as property that needs to be eliminated to make way for responsibility and care for the seeds and the knowledge that goes with them.

---

*(...continued)
recognizes the enormous contributions made by farmers worldwide in conserving and developing crop genetic resources. This constitutes the basis of Farmers' Rights. According to Article 9, governments are to protect and promote Farmers' Rights, but can choose the measures to do so according to their needs and priorities. Measures may include the protection of traditional knowledge, equitable benefit sharing, participation in decision-making, and the right to save, use, exchange and sell farm-saved seeds and propagating material. . . However, the understanding of Farmers' Rights and the modalities for their implementation is still vague."[65]

LAND RIGHTS

Having discussed food and seeds, we now need to dig into the ground under these, the land in which they grow. As with seeds, we have to consider whether land is just another commercial commodity, or something which we can hold but over which we cannot claim rights or ownership. And as with seeds, we need to discuss not only rights to land, but also the rights of the land. Put another way, is land simply a material substance definable by geographic boundaries, such as a building lot, a 'natural resource' waiting for human exploitation like Amazon forest or Alberta tar sands? Or can we think of land as Mother Earth, Pachamama? What can we say of rights to land if she is respected as our mother? As Marcelo Saavedra told me, "We Andean Indigenous Peoples don't really own the land or other Commons, rather, we belong to Pachamama ... An Inuk Elder once told me that being Inuit is being hunters. If you take away territory, you are affecting the hunter, therefore you are trying to exterminate Inuit. This simple reasoning applies to other Indigenous Peoples, for instance in the Amazon basin."[70] This is true in other traditional cultures. In Newfoundland, for example, people refer to the place they come from as the place they 'belong to'.

Advocacy for farmers' rights, or simple recognition of the traditional cultural practices of seed saving and selection, assumes that farmers have secure access to land from generation to generation. Food sovereignty also requires that farmers have secure access to land to grow food. But secure access and tenure does not necessarily imply or require rights to or ownership of land.

In North America, private property, and the supposed rights that come with it, are regarded as sacred, and among North American farmers, there has been a strongly held conviction that they have to own the land they work. Then they can get on with their farming, or so they think. In our capitalist system, their security, and for many – if not the majority – their 'pensions' lie in the land they own.

As with food, however, the right to land does not necessarily convey or provide for access, and title does not secure tenure – for example, when a bank holds the mortgage, giving it the right to foreclose and kick the farmer off the land if its terms are not met. The US mortgage meltdown in 2007-8 has made this painfully obvious not only to farmers, but to vast numbers of people who thought they owned their homes.

In fact, the ideology of ownership may be held responsible for a lack of security of tenure, as it leads farmers away from considering structures of land holding that would actually provide that security. This might be a long term lease, a land trust, communal holding or some other form, including, of course, individual ownership with no mortgage. One could say that the right of the land to be recognized and respected should come first, not the property rights of the landowner or speculator.

When we were farming (sheep and cattle, in Nova Scotia 1971-86) we needed to expand our land base to be economically viable. We were able to rent one farm (about 50 useful acres of pasture and hay land) from a

*retired dairy farmer at an affordable rate because he
wanted to see it farmed. The neighbouring farmer was
also retiring – with another 50 acres of pasture land, but
he wanted to sell the whole farm of 100 acres so he could
afford to build a small house for himself. We did not want
to buy and could not afford to buy. Fortunately the
provincial government instituted a land banking program
just at that time. We jumped at the opportunity and
arranged for the new provincial land bank to buy the
land which we then leased, with security of tenure as long
as we, or our heirs, wanted. The lease rent was fixed in
accordance with the agricultural value of the land. It all
made very good sense – until the Federation of Agriculture
insisted that the program had to include an option to buy.
The government gave in, changed the program
accordingly, and increased the rent to a commercial rate,
which we could not afford. Fortunately the provincial
government made provision for the few of us who had
been quick to take advantage of the program to continue
to rent at an agricultural rate. We considered ourselves to
be both fortunate and sensible in being able to continue
farming the land for an economic rent and, when we quit
farming, we simply turned the lease over to another
farmer. The land was no longer a market commodity.*

In the late 1980s the perennial 'farm crisis' in North
America expressed itself in a large number of farm
bankruptcies and foreclosures by the banks. The banks,
however, soon realized that they could not and did not want
to farm the land, so they leased it back to its previous owners,
who became tenants on their own land, without the security
they thought ownership would give them.

Twenty years later the issue of rights to land and land
ownership is paramount in southern Africa and South
America, though in quite different forms. It is, I believe, fair
to say that to a considerable extent the 'troubles' around

access to land and security of tenure in Africa arise from colonialism and its accompanying ideology of property and structures of land ownership on the one hand, and the drive by capital to gain control of 'natural resources' on the other. 'Natural resources' includes minerals, energy, water, biodiversity and land itself – frequently now for the growing of monoculture crops for agrofuel production.

The imposition of political boundaries on traditional unbounded grazing and agricultural lands – often described as territory, and certainly not as property – coupled with the granting of title to lands occupied, seized or otherwise acquired by the colonizers, not only broke up traditional communities but effectively destroyed their traditional pastoral livelihoods and ecologically sensible land tenure practices in their territory, not only in Africa but in North America as well. "Colonial governments perceived pastoral lands to be unoccupied (having no owner) or under-utilised and poorly managed thereby justifying their appropriation by the State and classification as government or Crown property."[71] Grazing lands and migratory corridors could be alienated without even informing pastoralists or local communities, and although these policies were initiated by colonial governments, they continued to be replicated by post-colonial governments. "This resulted in pastoral lands, formerly under the management of a particular clan or group, being divided amongst different administrative units."[72]

The territory of pastoral peoples, the borders of which had always been somewhat fluid, being subject to negotiation with neighbouring peoples, were converted into bounded properties.

The consequences of these colonial and post-colonial attitudes and practices manifest themselves in social instability resulting from immense inequities in land holding. South Africa is a prime example, where, after 13 years of supposed land reform, only about 4% of white-claimed agricultural land has been transferred and more than 80% of the South African land surface is still legally in the hands of whites. So entrenched is property ownership that now,

"the very Constitution that guarantees formal equality before the law also entrenches material inequality, especially in the distribution of land ownership. The entrenchment of the property clause in the Constitution is a major obstacle to the achievement of even the limited objectives of the land reform programme.... It is impossible to satisfy equally both the need to protect property rights and to ensure a policy of equitable distribution of land.... The recognition of property rights creates favourable conditions for property holders and their allies to contest expropriation in court. Under these circumstances, it is not surprising that the state is reluctant to use expropriation as a tool....

"Addressing the issue of a Bill of Rights on the eve of the collapse of apartheid in the late 1980s, Judge Didcott warned: 'What a Bill of Rights cannot afford to do here is to protect private property with such zeal that it entrenches privilege. A major problem which any future South African government is bound to face will be the problem of poverty, of its alleviation and of the need for the country's wealth to be shared more equitably'."[73]

This may serve as a healthy reminder that the lack of property 'protection' in the Canadian Charter of Rights and Freedoms is a fortunate omission.

Another lucid example of the conflict between property and the territory of communal holdings is the attempt to destroy the *ejidos* of Mexico. A similar process has been applied to the basic community units of the Andes, the *ayllul.*

Evangelina Robles, a lawyer who has represented the
Wirarika people of Mexico in hundreds of litigations to
recover their territory, describes how the 1917 Mexican
Constitution, adopted after the Revolution, recognized the
peoples' wish to have land seen as social property.[74] For the
indigenous communities, this meant legal recognition of the
ejido, or land held in common. In 1992, however, Article 27
of the Constitution was amended and a New Agrarian Law
brought with it the Program for the Certification of Ejido
Rights (PROCEDE). Officially, the objective of this program
was to give 'legal certainty' to members of the *ejidos* that they
had 'full possession' of the land. This was followed by the
Program for the Certification of Communal Rights
(PROCECOM) which applied the same 'legal certainty', i.e.
individual ownership, to indigenous land.

The first part of PROCEDE allows for the marking
out of communal land. The people were told by the state that
this would put them in a better position to resolve land
conflicts and territorial disputes with neighbouring communities. The second part of PROCEDE permits individuals
to have full property rights over their land, making it possible
for individuals to sell their plots. It also allows for the land to
be used as collateral for a loan from a bank or a money-
lender. Since decision-making power in both an *ejido* and an
indigenous community traditionally lay with the assembly,
which decided how land, water and forest should be used,
these private property provisions were a direct undercutting
of the power of the assembly.

"The government said the same thing about
PROCECOM and people still believed it. For instance,
indigenous communities that hadn't managed to get
the boundaries to their lands properly marked out
thought that they would achieve this through PROCE-
COM, and even though many people warned them
that it was a trick for privatising their land, the

communities continued to put their trust in the strength of their assemblies, and the *ejidos*, some of which were already weakened, thought that they could use the new program to regularize their situation and emerge stronger. But nothing worked out as they had hoped."[75]

"Individual rights can be rights that everyone has, such as human rights," says Robles, but "collective rights are those that a group of people has to decide how it wants to live, how it wants people to relate to each other. For example, a person can have the right to a piece of land on which to work and to live, but only a collective body, a community or a people, has the right to own that land and to decide what kind of life or civilisation should be practised on it. Individual rights have no meaning if they don't have a collective expression. For example, the right to education doesn't make sense unless a people decides what kind of education it wants."

"The right to territory isn't a property right, but the only way of getting legal recognition for territory is by turning it into property. For many indigenous communities, the relationship they have with their territory goes far beyond legal recognition ... For capitalism, the only kind of relationship that is possible is through property rights. It is capitalism that converts people's rights and their relationship with territory into property rights.... For communities, territory can only be seen as a whole – what you do with respect to one aspect of it is going to have repercussions for the other aspects. Everything is related – the people, the plants, the forests, everything. Territory is the place where you can still decide how to live, what to do. And there you can't separate the forest from the water, the land from the rainfall, and none of this from the customs of the communities....

For the Wixaritari Indians the very purpose of their life is to care for the world, this is their obligation. And only after this will come rights and benefits, but always linked to more obligations."[76]

Robles makes it clear that what the Mexican state offered the Wirarika people was not what the people thought they were getting. This could be attributed simply to a cultural misunderstanding: a fundamental difference in how peoples understand their relationship to the world about them and the place in which they live. What the people thought they were getting was jurisdiction, or a clearer definition of their territory. But property and territory do not share the same understanding of boundaries. Property is defined by its boundaries which transform it into a viable commodity. A territory is defined more by its use and characteristics and peoples' relationships with it than by strict, identifiable boundaries; the lack of clear boundaries may require inter-community negotiation and good will, actually strengthening communal holdings.

The treatment of indigenous peoples in North America by the European and British colonizers and settlers bears an unhappy resemblance to the Mexican treatment of indigenous peoples. Their 'settlement' on the land, in part because it was unbounded – unmarked and unfenced – was not recognized, nor was their traditional hunting, trapping or gathering territory. Thus land inhabited – settled – by hunter-gatherers, as in New England, was not recognized as owned by anyone in the eyes of the colonizers. The only land that the English settlers recognized as 'owned' – and to which the natives could claim 'rights' – were the gardens which were visibly and effectively fenced – to keep the wild creatures out.[77]

The colonials consequently felt they could just help themselves to this 'vacant' land and push the natives into small areas designated as 'reserves' – that is, land generously set aside for those natives that did not die of white men's diseases. In some cases the natives were simply hunted down and eliminated in order to clear the land.

Bruce Chatwin, in writing about 'outback' Australia, describes a strikingly similar scenario in a totally different climate.

"White men ... made the common mistake of assuming that, because the Aboriginals were wanderers, they could have no system of land tenure. This was nonsense. Aboriginals, it was true, could not imagine territory as a block of land hemmed in by frontiers: but rather as an interlocking network of 'lines' or 'ways through'.

"For this there was one simple explanation. Most of Outback Australia was arid scrub or desert where rainfall was always patchy and where one year of plenty might be followed by seven years of lean. To move in such a landscape was survival: to stay put in the same place suicide. The definition of a man's 'own country' was 'the place in which I do not have to ask'. Yet to feel 'at home' in that country depended on being able to leave it. Everyone hoped to have at least four 'ways out', along which he could travel in a crisis. Every tribe – like it or not – had to cultivate relations with his neighbour."[78]

In the north of Canada the situation was more extreme, in keeping with the climate, and the fur traders that found their way north were dependent for survival on the Indigenous peoples (Inuit and Indian) who were essentially nomadic hunters and trappers. The white man could not discern the territory on which they lived or how they related to it and occupied it.[79]

The white man's lack of discernment did not, however, stop first the King of England and then the colonials from claiming and settling land in this unknown territory.

Indian and Northern Affairs Canada provides an official view of this process:

"The last of the wars between France and England raged for 7 years. The fortress of Louisbourg fell in 1758. Québec, the heart of New France fell the year after. At the end of the war King George the III of England issued the Royal Proclamation of 1763. It confirmed that a vast area in the interior of North American was Indian country and would be preserved as hunting grounds for the Indians. The Eastern boundary was formed by the Appalachian mountains, the Western boundary was left undefined. King George ordered that no one could use these lands without the public permission of the Indians themselves. And only the Crown or its authorized representatives, he said, could actually acquire the land if indeed the Indians were willing to part with it. From this point on, the British Crown would be the central agent in the transfer of Indian lands to colonial settlers."[80]

This all sounds very respectful and even fair until one considers the circumstances defined by the colonials under which the Indians would be "willing to part with it". Not until 1997 were hard definitions as to what aboriginal rights and title actually meant under Canadian law laid down. That year the Supreme Court of Canada heard the case generally referred to as Delgamuukw in which the Gitxsan and Wet'suwet'en people claimed that pre-existing (that is, prior to the King of England decree) Indigenous rights and title to their traditional territory in BC had not been extinguished.

"The court said that aboriginal title is a right to the land itself. Until this decision, no Canadian court had so directly addressed the definition of aboriginal title. Other cases had dealt with aboriginal rights in terms of the right to use the land for traditional purposes such as hunting.

Aboriginal title is a property right that goes much further than aboriginal rights of usage.... In many ways, aboriginal title is just like ordinary land ownership. The owner can exclude others from the property, extract resources from it, use it for business or pleasure. But there are important differences, too.

○ Aboriginal title is a communal right. An individual cannot hold aboriginal title. This means that decisions about land must be made by the community as a whole.

○ Because aboriginal title is based on a First Nation's relationship with the land, these lands cannot be used for a purpose inconsistent with that continuing relationship ...

○ Aboriginal title lands can be sold only to the federal government.

○ Aboriginal title has the additional protection of being a constitutional right."[81]

The story, unfortunately, hardly ends there. Negotiation can go on forever, and may well do so. In the meantime, Indigenous peoples across Canada struggle to recover their traditional ways, particularly in food and language, hoping their land claims will actually be recognized and settled justly.

Lurking behind all of the situations described above is the apparent inability of western society to recognize peoples and nations as social units. Worldwide, imperialists and colonizers have been unable – or perhaps unwilling even if able – to observe how people live, not as individuals, but as members of a clan, tribe or nation and to respect them as such. In western minds there seem to be only individuals and states. It is then logical for human rights to be individualistic while sovereignty is granted only to states (though not without qualification, as we will see later in discussing the right to intervene.) It is thus not surprising that the Canadian state has great difficulty in dealing with Indigenous peoples and nations.

In 2008, access to and control of land for food and agrofuel production became a prominent global issue when commodity prices, including for food, oil and synthetic fertilizers, shot up. Many countries realized how vulnerable their food sources were, and speculators and 'investors' were looking for a safe place to put their money in the face of the deepening financial meltdown. All of a sudden, so it appeared, 'vacant' or 'under-utilized' land with any agricultural potential became an essential investment for a wide range of 'food insecure' countries, including China, Saudi Arabia and Korea, as well as an investment opportunity for agrofuel production.[82]

In defense of their land grabs, one could almost hear the states, sovereign wealth funds and speculators preparing their moral argument for the right to food for their populations, and hence the need for the land base with which to address this need, along with a legal argument that they have the right to purchase land since it is nothing more than an under-utilized resource or commodity in their eyes. One could also hear them trying to make the argument that their use of the land would be more 'responsible' than its use by subsistence farmers and pastoralists because it would be more 'productive', even if it meant starvation – or death – for the farmers displaced by big machines and monoculture, as in Brazil with the advance of sugarcane for the production of ethanol, or the destruction of the Amazonian rain forest to make way for cattle destined for export as beef.

RIGHTS AND RESOURCES:
FROM CREATION TO COMMODITY

If 'natural resources', including food, land, fossil fuels and water were actually infinite – as assumed by the imperative of economic growth and the ideological notions of technological progress and sustainable development – then one might be able to argue that the privatization of these 'resources' through expropriation and commodification is tolerable. Everyone might then be able to claim some portion as their own, without, at least theoretically, depriving others of their share. The legal term for this is *non-rivalous*: i.e., my use of the resource – referring usually to an *idea* in copyright law – does not diminish yours. Like skating on the lake in our neighbourhood, the more the merrier; and while it may get crowded on Sunday afternoon, the same amount of ice will still be there when everyone has gone home for supper. The assertion of rights to water, land or food would be redundant, or irrelevant – irrelevant, that is, until the ideology of ownership, capital and accumulation moves in.

As we saw earlier, Locke made this assumption that there was enough for all – provided that no one took more than he or she could personally use. One could see, for example, Locke's assumption describing the picking of wild blackberries in southern British Columbia today or gathering cod in the North Atlantic fifty years ago. There is no reason to think, however, that Locke, three centuries ago, intended to lay the philosophical foundation for the limitless claims of transnational corporations to what its employees have extracted from nature (the earth and its elements and creatures), whether it be iron ore, oil, gold, fish or human and non-human DNA, as theirs by right. Yet this is the absurd situation today.

To mask the brutality of contemporary claims to what can be extracted from the *state of nature* and claimed as property and owned, the term 'natural resources' has been introduced. It is a term which appears to be free of any religious or theological implications or obligations. Resources and rights are, in this view, equally 'natural' and therefore beyond question. (A Native elder introduced me to the more accurate term 'elements', rather than 'resources', in referring to the constituents of Creation.)

Natural resources are not, however, limitless, contrary to the carefree blindness with which we consume fossil fuels and fresh water in our version of development. Furthermore, using the term 'resources' suggests that value adheres only to that which is available for our exploitation and which is mixed with the labour or capital of the person (natural or artificial) which then becomes its owner. Nature/Creation, is not recognized as having any intrinsic value. Owning, then, is simply a natural right since it is I, we, or the inanimate persona of the corporation that give value to these resources, which are then 'value-added'. French sociologist Bruno Latour provides a refreshingly skewed perspective on these assumptions as he turns the subject right around, saying that the elements of nature can no longer be regarded as simply a means utilized to satisfy human desires, but must be regarded as of intrinsic value, entities in their own right.

"Ecological crises ... present themselves as *generalized revolts of the means;* no entity – whale river, climate, earthworm, tree, calf, cow, pig, brood – agrees any longer to be treated 'simply as a means' but always insists on being treated 'always also as an end.' ... it is rather the simple consequence of the disappearance of the notion of external nature."[83]

The Market Economy requires the commodification of everything that is designated as a 'resource' – *human resources* as well as natural resources – so that it can be owned and traded, thus establishing its 'value' – market value, that is. The 'value' that is 'added' by the worker (miner, butcher, field hand) who actually transforms that resource into a product is claimed (appropriated) by the owner. This is clearly a perversion of the labour theory of value (and a grand distortion of both Locke and Marx) as, in the current corporate world, the owners are, in their capacity of shareholders, neither entrepreneurs nor workers, yet they lay claim to the value added. Functionally, they are simply parasites.*[84] The 'value' they add, unlike that of the worker or peasant farmer, is fictional, but nevertheless financially 'real' and bankable. Just ask any bank or business CEO who receives millions of dollars in 'compensation' – at least until very recently – what they are actually 'compensated' for.**[85]

---

* "One does not see rising employee income as a measure of corporate success. Indeed, gains to employees are losses to the corporation. And this betrays an unconscious bias: that employees are not really part of the corporation. They have no claim on the wealth they create, no say in governance, and no vote for the board of directors. They're not citizens of corporate society, but subjects ... The oddity of it all is veiled by the incantation of a single magical word: ownership. Because we say shareholders own corporations, they are permitted to contribute very little, and take quite a lot."[83]

** In early 2009 Nortel Networks, once a major Canadian employer (15,000 in Ottawa alone) was in bankruptcy proceedings when it
(continued...)

As mentioned in the previous chapter, in numerous colonial situations the colonizers felt it appropriate to seize land that they considered as not really owned because it was not being sufficiently worked by whoever might claim to be the owner. The natives, that is, were not entitled – had no rights – to the land because they were not adequately exploiting the 'resources' in their care, nor did they have title to it since it was most likely communally held and there was no land registry in place, if only because there was no state to create one. This is also the situation today, where the only form of agriculture recognized as legitimate by the dominant culture of the west is intensive industrial agricultural production. Pastoralism and subsistence are not recognized as valid and legitimate (valuable) relationships to the land and can, therefore, be eliminated to make way for more 'efficient' and 'productive' use of the 'resource' (land). As Marcelo Saavedra-Vargas said to me, this is breaking the link with Pachamama, or freeing the peasant to become hired labour on the industrial plantation imposed on the land.

In Latin America and elsewhere we now see a similar pattern of land appropriation where peasant farmers and forest dwellers are being driven off the land which feeds them by big landowners expanding the industrial production of soy beans and corn, genetically engineered and patented, for ethanol production and feed for intensive livestock operations in Europe. This is a vastly different vocation for the land than its natural provision of food, medicines, building materials and firewood for subsistence farmers and peasants.

**(...continued)
announced that its senior executives would get $45 million in bonuses to save the company. These are the same executives that supervised the corporation's descent into bankruptcy. According to the plan, the top 1000 executives would get an average bonus of $45,000 each while the balance of the company's North American workforce of about 20,000 would get $150 each.[84]

With this attitude, the possibility of mutuality is unrecognized and excluded. Perhaps it is these 'resources' that own us. How else should we describe our dependency on fossil fuels? Can it not be said that our automobiles own us, that is, that they determine the shape of much of our lives? Is it not also true that in the highly industrialized societies we are owned by the supermarkets as far as our food supply is concerned? Only a small – although growing – percentage of the population in these societies actually own their own food system in the sense of being in control of it (growing, harvesting, preparing). Most inhabitants of the industrialized states (peculiarly identified as the 'developed' countries) are utterly dependent on the global corporate food system over which we have absolutely no control and from which we can expect no security either as gardeners and farmers or as the public ('consumers'). We have no rights in or to this system.

In a sense, we have mystified *natural resources* and given them infinite capacity, energy and power. If they are also regarded as if infinite in supply, they can have no market value. To have market value requires scarcity. To create scarcity, these limitless natural elements require *enclosure* and commodification. Hence the need for carefully demarcated property lines or description and legal title, whether that be in the form of title to land, a mineral claim, or a water right.

This logic also applied in the distinctly non-natural realm of patents until very recently; discoveries could not be patented, only inventions (products and processes). Similarly, the principle of copyright is that ideas, regarded as unbounded, limitless and thus non-rivalrous, cannot be copyrighted, but the *expression* of an idea can be owned and copyrighted.

In recent years, however, there has been an escalating push by the corporate sector for an expansion of the definition of property which can be 'protected' by various forms of rights, such as life forms (including genetic material and seeds – referred to and demeaned as 'plant genetic re-sources'), computer code, procedures of genetic engineering, databases and, of course, pharmaceuticals. In other words, in the minds of capital, the claims of ownership rights appear to be without limit – just like the assumption that there are unlimited 'natural resources'.

RIGHT TO WATER

"All waters are a sacred gift from the Creator and a
precious birth-right of all living beings. All waters are
part of a singular network of life – the great oceans and
seas, the frozen waters and glaciers, the cosmic sea
from which are born the clouds, snow and rains that
nurture the plants, animals, birds, fishes, insects, rep-
tiles and humankind. We are of waters and waters are
of us."*

Like 'right to food' and 'right to land', 'right to water' has
become an increasingly frequent battle cry for social justice
around the world; but like the others, this claim raises
fundamental questions about the nature of these elements
and the possibility of owning them, as well as access and
distribution. Water is probably the most difficult to deal
with. Not only does it share with food the characteristic of
being not just a human need but an absolute necessity, and
with land the character of being what the Romans called *res
divini juris*, things 'unownable' (of divine jurisdiction)

---

* from the invitation to the Hopi - Azteca Dance Ceremony Celebrating
Water, 4th World Water Forum, Mexico City, 2006

because of their sacred nature,*[86] but, as mentioned earlier, water has the unique distinction of never standing still. It only stands still, neither flowing away nor evaporating, when it is captured and bounded, by a *watertight* container (as in plastic bottle – or legal argument).

Maybe it is this 'flow' characteristic, this constant and often unseen movement of water, which most clearly marks water as *res divini juris*. There are certainly millions of Indigenous peoples around the world for whom water is sacred (the blood of Mother Earth), and for whom its availability for human use is a social responsibility extending far beyond the immediate human community. However, the idea, to say nothing of the belief, that water is sacred is alien to western rationalist, reductionist thought.

Thinking of water as a human right itself alters the character of water, turning it into a 'natural resource' to be managed for human benefit. But the questions of anthropocentrism and individualism remain unaddressed by the advocates of the right to water. As geography professor Karen Bakker emphasizes,

"the anthropocentrism of human rights fails to recognize rights of non-humans (or ecological rights). Providing a human right to water may, ironically, imply the further degradation of hydrological systems upon which ecosystems (and, of course, human beings) depend.

"The framework of human rights is also individualistic and legalistic, and hence can not address the complex, collective governance issues which constrain

---

* As Carol Rose points out, "The things classed under this rubric in Roman law—temples, tombs, religious statuary—were considered to belong to no one because they were dedicated to the service of the gods, or because an offense to them was considered to be offensive to the gods. Such things were a class of *res nullius* because although they are physically capable of appropriation, they are still unowned; the impediment to propertization is not natural but divine."[85]

access to water at the urban scale. The equitable
provision of water supply necessarily implies a degree
of solidarity (both physical and material). Yet is
precisely this notion of solidarity which human rights,
in isolation, can not provide."[87]

'Water for all' and a 'human right to water' are clearly
expressions of two very different ways of viewing the world.

Perhaps the image of an hourglass can help visualize
the bigger picture of water. On the one side, or at the top, is
the large catchment area from which we withdraw water. It
then passes through some amount of piping, including our
own internal plumbing, and then through more piping and
out into a large discharge area – which may be the river from
which it was drawn in the first place. What this picture
illustrates is that we cannot think individualistically about a
right to water. It has to be social, it has to be ecological. It
requires a water ethic that is strong on responsibility
unlimited in time and space – "to the seventh generation".

We humans may have a claim for access to water, but
we cannot responsibly place ourselves ahead of all the other
creatures, the flora and fauna whose habitation we share but
whose voices have no place in our structures of governance.
Nor can we assume to have the authority to claim or grant
ownership of water or rights to water (water rights), in spite
of a long-held assumption in North America that government, whether referring to a municipal, provincial, state or
national government, has such authority. Only in the fast-
fading thirty year neo-liberal era has a contrary assumption
– that the private sector can exercise such authority –
contested the public (state) model. But as Bakker points out,
this imposed binary may exclude more adequate and just
forms of 'governance':

"Pursuit of a campaign to establish water as a human
right risks reinforcing the public/private binary upon
which this confrontation is predicated, occluding

possibilities for collective action beyond corporatist models of service provision. In contrast, the "alter-globalization" debate opened up by disrupting the public/private binary has created space for the construction of alternative community economies of water."[88]

As I have emphasized throughout this book, there is a great deal more to the language of rights than a moral statement or a legal claim. In India, for example, access to and uses of water have always been crucial and complex issues, given the dramatically different character of the land from region to region and the country's very complex social structure and its political history.

"India has no real laws to govern the use of groundwater for either communities or industry. Groundwater disputes in India are settled according to the Indian Easements Act of 1882, in which ground-water is interpreted as a right attached to land. Hence, owners of a plot of land have unrestricted access to the water that lies below it. While such an interpretation offers a degree of independence to individual and community users, the same law has been used to justify the sucking out of millions of litres of water by giant industries every day. The growth of bottling and paper industries, distilleries and steel plants has resulted in pitched battles between communities and corporations for control over common water sources."[89]

"Farmers near Plachimada in the southern Indian state of Kerala, where a huge Coca-Cola plant is located, have accused Coke of parching and polluting their villages. In December, 2003, the high court in the state capital, Thiruvananthapuram, ruled that the village council, or *panchayat*, had the right to deny the company access to groundwater to protect farmers. The court ordered the company to find other sources, defining groundwater as a national resource. In a further blow to Coke, a Supreme Court monitoring committee visited Plachimada last August [2004] and ordered the company to retrieve all of its waste from farmers' land and ensure that all those living around the plant had access to clean water. The committee said that since the factory opened, groundwater had become unfit for drinking."[90]

Higher courts subsequently overturned the state court's judgements on technical grounds, while recognizing the importance of the issue.

Water is rare and precious for the millions of rural refugees crowded around the cities of the south in slums and *favelas* who live without sewers and without clean water or water only from a distant standpipe, while they can see the rich watering their lawns and filling their swimming pools; the millions who live by polluted streams and rivers that provide their only water for washing, drinking and watering their crops; the millions displaced by big dams to provide electricity to the urban wealthy; the millions affected by the mines and mills that pollute whatever water they can access; and the millions of women around the world who spend much of their day carrying water from a distant source for their gardens and families.

At the same time, for most people in the north water is clean, ubiquitous and free. That is what it was for us on our farm in Nova Scotia (appropriately called Brookland), whether it was the water from our shallow well or from the stream below the garden. The only expense associated with it was the electricity to power the pumps and, very infrequently, the cost of a new pump. A shortage of water was not the issue, though too much of it in the form of rain sometimes was. Given that we had only one neighbour upstream, and none downstream for miles, we did not have to concern ourselves with being cut off upstream or depriving anyone downstream of water. Our situation could not have been more different than that of farmers in the arid regions of India.

Now in Ottawa our water situation is different again. The road where we live was rebuilt from the bottom up recently. Buried deep below the roadway were the ageing pipes for sewage, storm sewer and fresh water that needed to be replaced, with the aid of very big and very costly machines – and some highly skilled workers. I was a fascinated spectator as the work progressed down the street and finished right outside my window. As the road was opened up, it was very impressive to see the original pipes that had required a great deal of manpower and meant trenching and tunneling through solid rock in many places some 70-100 years ago. All this work, then and now, was to ensure that we surface dwellers would have a plenteous, reliable supply of clean water. We expect it to be there, 24 hours a day, every day. But is that our right? Or is it an extreme privilege and blessing? Are we grateful, or do we take it for granted – the pipes, the pumping and the water itself – that the endless supply of clean water is all a municipal responsibility for which we do nothing more than pay a very small tax to the city.

Many people who enjoy a secure supply of clean water may be quick to condemn Venezuela's President Chavez, but it would seem more appropriate to applaud his move to "change the vocation of the land" from producing packaging materials to producing food and conserving water:

Venezuela has taken over a 3700 acre eucalyptus farm owned by cardboard packaging manufacturer Smurfitt Kappa of Ireland. President Chavez said the government had taken over the El Pinal eucalyptus plantation because the water-hungry trees were drying out local rivers. He said the government would "use the wood in a rational manner and then we will change the vocation of the land. We are going to plant other things that are not eucalyptus." Smurfitt Kappa owns 74,000 acres in Venezuela.[91]

Unfortunately, the calls for recognition of a universal human right to water do not address the question of whether water is something that can be identified, bounded, commodified and owned, or a sacred natural element, the 'Mother Earth' of which we are all composed, which courses through our bodies like it courses through Pachamama. (The 'hydrological cycle' is a rather less poetic – though perhaps more 'scientific'– term.)

Of course water can be captured – by a dam, a rain barrel, a pump in a well, diversion of a river, an irrigation canal – and then it can be measured and traded, but the infrastructure – the pumps, pipes and filtration systems – have to be paid for, one way or another, and the questions of how it is distributed (the water infrastructure), to whom and in what quantities all have to be addressed, along with the question of how the costs of distribution are to be covered. As Karen Bakker elegantly put it, "How are we to adjudicate the best means of organizing our metabolism of water?"

The control of water through ownership of the supply-distribution system may really amount to *de facto* ownership of the water itself unless there is a strong regulatory regime in place to ensure that the distribution system serves the public good and provides water for all. But then one also has to consider who owns the location of the source, or access to the source – the well, dam, irrigation ditch or pipe into the river.

All of these questions should be addressed before any claim of a right to water is made. Otherwise it is too easy for a wealthy elite to monopolize both the sources and the delivery of water through political control of the state (town, city, province, national government) in a public system, through privately owned systems, or Public-Private

Partnerships (P3s). If these questions are not addressed it is also all too easy for Coca-Cola, or any other corporation – particularly given that corporations have the legal rights of persons – to claim its right to water along with the subsistence farmer or a thirsty child. Similarly a state may authorize the construction of a dam by a mining company to produce the electrical power to operate their smelter and consequently affect the water supply of every inhabitant downstream.

But whose water is it? In British Columbia we had a water license which came with the deed to the land. The license, which was granted by the Provincial Government for a negligible fee, gave us the legal right to draw water from the small stream running (now underground) through our farm. The province was *de facto* owner of the water, and empowered to grant water rights (licenses) in the constitutional arrangements between the Federal Government of Canada and the provinces. However, when we had to drill a new deep well, no permission was needed for access to far more water than that provided by the licensed stream.

We also had a neighbour – on the other side of the mountain – who had a flock of dairy sheep from which he made excellent cheese. He fought a losing battle with a family that moved in above him and diverted, for their own use, the stream that supplied his water. The provincial government, supposedly responsible for water management, proved to be useless in enforcing his water license. (He finally sold out and moved.) A similar scenario could describe any number of irrigation projects and water systems around the world, in both deserts and mountains.

Here in Ottawa we get a monthly bill for water and sewage based on the amount of water we use, but is this bill actually for the water or the infrastructure of treatment plants, pumps and pipes that delivers it to us? If the water is coming from the Ottawa River that runs through the city, certainly the water cannot be owned by the city, or by its residents. The river has its origins far away, flows through the city, and on down to the ocean, supplying many other communities along the way.

There are laws concerning the city's responsibility for water quality for its residents, and also for the city's sewage, for the sake of those living downstream, but there is no system of allocation of the river water (water rights) for the communities and industries located along it. Fortunately this is not an issue, given the volume of water in the river – but this could well change as the climate changes. Another unaddressed issue is the effect of water usage and quality on the surrounding ecosystem, which might well protest in predictable and unpredictable ways the violation of *its* water rights.

Similar questions can be asked about the water being drawn from a large aquifer. However, rainwater falls from the sky on a particular location. So it might be reasonable to say that the people in that location have a right to that water, but then, what happens next month, or next year, when there might not be any rain? The community's right to water becomes an empty dream, or a dry standpipe.

Jurisdictional issues over access to water may arise locally, around a small stream, but such issues become of extreme importance where there are trans-boundary flows of rivers, for example the Columbia River flowing from British Columbia into Washington state or the Red River flowing from North Dakota into Manitoba, the Ganges river in the Indian subcontinent, or the Parana-Paraguay river system in South America. Obviously any absolute claim to a specific amount of water has the possibility of turning into an international conflict, if not war.

So now we have to recognize four components of the right to water: the water itself, access to the water and the means of its distribution, its end use, and where it goes from there (sewers, evaporation, rivers...).

It is said that oil and water do not mix, but they are beginning to share other characteristics – or at least they were until the financial meltdown of 2008-9. Commodity markets have long been a place of active trading in oil and gas stocks, but there has been little interest in water stocks. This may now be changing, like the climate. The authoritative business news service, Bloomberg, reported that "the world's biggest investors are choosing water as the commodity that may appreciate the most in the next several decades." Between 2003 and 2006, the Bloomberg world water index of 11 utilities returned 35% annually, compared with 29% for Bloomberg's oil and gas stock index and 10% for the Standard & Poor's 500-stock index.[92]

According to Bloomberg, Belgium's richest man, Albert Frère, has a $3.4-billion investment in water and energy through his stake in Suez SA, the world's second-biggest owner of water utilities. A vice-president of Suez said, a few years ago, "We now agree that water is a public asset and should not be appropriated by the private sector. Water is a public service and that belongs to everyone. All people should have the right to water, but we need to transform that right into a reality."[93] Of course Suez would rather not pay for the water it distributes. If water is a right, it can claim it should be free while Suez makes its profit from building and operating the distribution infrastructure as a monopoly with state support.

Then there is Dallas hedge fund manager and oil billionaire Boone Pickens, who spent more than $50-million for water rights around his ranch in North Texas and says he has enough water to serve 20 per cent of the Dallas-Fort Worth area. So far, however, Pickens has failed to convince any Texas cities to buy his water, and he needs a commitment before he can build a $2-billion pipeline system.[94]

The pitch for trading in water is getting more sophisticated, as indicated by this website message:

"Clean fresh water isn't a commodity. At least not like oil or wheat are commodities. That's because you CAN live without oil or wheat. But you can't go more than a few days without water. More importantly, most commodities are easily replaced... You can substitute coal or natural gas for oil. You can substitute corn or oats for wheat. But what can the human body use in place of water? What can our food crops drink instead? – nothing. So water is a necessity, not a commodity... Something necessary to human life yet ignored by the investing public...that sounds like an appealing opportunity, doesn't it?... There is no shortage of water... but there is an acute shortage of CLEAN, potable water... So invest in water and you invest in a certain future... you can ride the water rush by grabbing shares of this one stock: XXX is a basket woven of water utilities, pipe makers, pump makers, filter manufacturers, water treatment companies, general water infrastructure, and water testing and analysis."[95]

This is an interesting approach, since it sidesteps altogether the difficult questions about water, such as whether or not it can be owned and whether it is sacred or just a 'natural resource'. It avoids the notion of a right to water and simply states that it is a human necessity. It is the delivery infrastructure that is the object of investment, and managed effectively, control of the distribution infrastructure can provide effective control of, and profit from, water.

"An alternative vision focuses on the tension between individual access and collective control, rather than between public and private management. It suggests that the notion of 'public trust' (and the approach to property rights that this implies) is a useful way of resolving some of the key issues in the debate. In this way community forms of water management have a greater potential to be appropriately inclusive and environmentally sustainable."[96]

As I have said before, much of the discussion about water, and the right to water, revolves around technical/ technological means of control and distribution of water; in other words, trying to find a technical or technological solution for a social problem. "Community forms of water management" can only be created on a collective, social foundation and a community acceptance of responsibility.

RIGHTS OF NATURE:
PLANTS, ANIMALS, FISH

One of the premises of the language of rights is the anthropocentric conviction of western civilization that the world revolves around humans. The consequence is that when concern is expressed about the ways animals are treated, as in factory farming or the abuse of pets, it is in terms of humane or inhumane treatment, as if the only ethical or moral standards were human. The issue is not, apparently, one of respect for the animals themselves and their integrity.

Indeed, it appears that animal rights advocates need to create a category of animals which have at least some characteristics that can be identified as human in order to be able to assign them rights which are then to be respected and enforced by the state. For example, Tom Regan, an early and prolific advocate of animal rights and author of *The Case for Animal Rights,* says, after much academic argument, that rights apply to "mentally normal mammals of a year or more". These then are given the special status of "subjects-of-a-life," a status they share with humans. He goes on to say that "both human and nonhuman subjects-of-a-life, in my view, have a basic moral right to respectful treatment."[97] The line he draws between those non-human animals that qualify for rights and those that do not is that "some nonhuman animals resemble normal humans in morally relevant ways. In particular, they bring the mystery of a unified psychological presence to the world."[98]

Despite his lengthy argument, where Regan draws his magic line appears to me as singularly arbitrary and slippery, as it depends entirely on a human description and perception of a "psychological presence". I would prefer to respect and explore diversity and not draw a line. Or, as Bruno Latour puts it,

"It is clearer now: the extension of the collective makes possible a presentation of humans and non-humans that is completely different from the one required by the cold war between objects and subjects.... Humans and non-humans can join forces without requiring their counterparts on the other side to disappear. To put it another way: objects and subjects can never associate with one another; humans and non-humans can.... Non-humans are not defined by necessity any more than they are defined by mute objectivity. The only thing that can be said about them is that they emerge in surprising fashion, lengthening the list of beings that must be taken into account."[99]

After more philosophical argument, Regan offers a view of what it means to have a right: "To have a right is to be in a position to claim, or to have claimed on one's behalf, that something is due or owed, and the claim that is made is a claim made against somebody.... To make a claim ... is to assert that one is oneself entitled, or that someone else is entitled, to treatment of a certain kind and that the treatment is due or owed directly to the individual(s) in question. To make a claim thus involves both claims-to and claims-against."[100]

The unequivocal individualism expressed by Regan suggests that his view of society is simply "many individuals", or, in terms of my earlier diagram, lots of dots. For Regan, the "paradigmatic rights-holders are individuals".[101] He does admit, however, that the individualistic nature of moral rights makes it difficult to reconcile rights with the holistic view of nature characteristic of environmental ethics.

Regan's final word on animal rights seems to come down to this: "The principle basic moral right possessed by all moral agents and patients is the right to respectful treatment."[102] In plainer speaking, I would simply say that the moral 'claim' of animals, without qualification, is for respect. The ethical treatment of all creatures, then, should be one of respect for all of Mother Earth's children – plants, animals and fish – as well as a sense of affinity (a shared space in the world) with them.

While living in wet southern British Columbia some years ago I had a number of small warts on my hands. A long-time resident told me that slugs were good for warts. Up to then, all I could see in slugs were voracious consumers of my strawberries. I had to overcome my distaste for slugs by picking one up in my fingers and placing it on a wart, while telling it to be a good little slug and stay put long enough to do some good. I think I tried two or three slugs in that first treatment. Some slugs are more effective than others, it seems. To my surprise, the wart quietly withdrew – disappeared! So I treated the other warts and they too disappeared. Now I have to restrain myself from wanting to pet the slimy little creatures out of appreciation for their contribution to the public good.

Respect for animals obviously has its implications for Intensive Livestock Operations, i.e., factory farms or industrial meat and egg production (and much of aquaculture must be included in this category). There is no ethical/moral rationalization possible for these facilities which treat their victims, and their human workers, not with respect but as production machines to be run as 'efficiently' as possible in order to maximize profit as a link in the corporately-controlled industrial food system. Of course there are many operators of such facilities who do have qualms about what they are doing, but these are overcome by the requirement to be competitive in the marketplace in order to make a living. So you either play the game or get out; and maybe start over with pastured pigs and a big garden, the one you never had time for as an industrial farmer.

This pressure to produce, by whatever industrial means necessary, is generally justified as the only way to feed the hungry of the world. Certainly the industrial food sector, and particularly companies such as Monsanto and Syngenta which are ruthlessly pushing genetically engineered crops around the world, are claiming that their 'modern' food production systems are the answer to feeding a growing global population without destroying the environment.

One of the greatest contributors to the welfare of and respect for farm animals has been Temple Grandin, an autistic who has turned her 'disability' (the drug companies now try to define autism as a 'disease') into a gift by using her extreme sensitivity to feel the world as a cow might, and to understand what the animal finds reassuring or threatening. Virtually singlehandedly, Grandin has transformed livestock handling from the rough application of force, including the electric cattle prod, in facilities designed with humans in mind, to a process that respects the senses of the animal: sight lines, odours, light and dark, rounded passageways and smooth surfaces. I'm not aware that she ever talks about animal rights.

Grandin's approach challenges western anthropo-centrism, which keeps us as humans abstracted from the environment we actually inhabit and which inhabits us. We may say that we are responsible – as co-creators, as stewards, even as curators – but these attitudes still express a distanced responsibility reflecting human alienation and exceptionalism, if not superiority.

Fortunately, this anthropocentrism is being challenged – not just by some animal welfare advocates and philosophers, but also by thoughtful scientists, naturalists and farmers within western societies whose understanding of the human is simply expressed in the book title, *One Animal Among Many*.[103] Of course such thinking – not about animals' rights, but about respect for all creatures and our place among them – is not new. It has always been an essential characteristic of many cultures and peoples and remains central to Indigenous identities.

The idea that rights are inherent in human beings, that human rights are natural, inalienable attributes of human and somehow set humans apart from all other creatures is a form of exceptionalism that has caused, and continues to cause, incredible damage to the world and its inhabitants. 'Man' is not a unique beast, just different and, perhaps, more dangerous than all the others. This need not be regarded as demeaning. As Donna Haraway has written, "It's a deep pleasure being one among many living and dying creatures, and to understand that walking away from human exceptionalism is as much a relief from carrying on a kind of impossible fantasy as it is a burden to take it on."[104]

Elaborating on the term 'exceptionalism', Haraway explains that "The dominant western philosophical and scientific traditions have emphasized the exceptional nature of human beings. Since the 18th century Enlightenment, what constitutes the human is its difference from all the 'others' – from gods, demons, creepy-crawlies, blobs, slaves and, above all, animals. The relentless quest for something that creates a gap between what's human and what's not, that's human exceptionalism."

When we were sheep farmers, I had a working dog – my inseparable partner for a decade. Jule lived to work. She loved to show off her skill and we used to do demonstrations of sheep handling at the county fair. She slept in our unheated back porch and virtually never came into the house. As she lost her youthful vigour she became more cunning in how she managed the sheep in order to conserve her energy – and the sheep, having grown up with her, had learned to respect her and take her 'eye' seriously. (This was mutual, as a good dog does not excite or cause fear in the sheep – unless they get obstreperous.) She became more arthritic until one day, after we had sold the sheep and there was nothing for her to do, we came home to find her lying outside the back door under a drip from the roof. We took her in and warmed her up, but she just wanted to lie in her customary place in the back porch. As I sat on the doorstep she told me with her eyes that she was through with life. There was a brief family discussion about taking her to the vet. I said no. I said she had made her will quite clear to me. We respected her decision and she died peacefully that night in her usual position on the mat in the back porch.

A very refreshing attitude is now being articulated in what gets referred to as 'the rights of Nature' by people and peoples who have a very different self-understanding and starting point. For example, in the new constitution of Ecuador[105] it is not human rights or the rights of an individual that comes first, but an affirmation of Pachamama, of life itself.

The new constitution was proclaimed in Spanish and Quechua, the two official languages of Ecuador, but it would appear that it was composed in Spanish, given the language of the English translation (the Spanish *derechos* is rights in English, but there is no word for rights in Quechua). It was prepared with the assistance of a non-profit organization in the USA that has been helping jurisdictions in the US "that recognize that environmental protection cannot be attained under a structure of law that treats natural ecosystems as property."

"Over the past year, the Community Environmental Legal Defense Fund has assisted the Ecuadorian Constituent Assembly to develop and draft provisions for the new constitution to put ecosystem rights directly into the Ecuadorian constitution. The elected Delegates to the Constituent Assembly requested that the Legal Defense Fund draft language based on ordinances developed and adopted by municipalities in the US where it has assisted more than a dozen local municipalities with drafting and adopting local laws recognizing Rights of Nature."[106]

Article One of Ecuador's new constitution states that, "Nature or Pachamama, where life is reproduced and exists, has the right to exist, persist, maintain and regenerate its vital cycles, structure, functions and its processes in evolution."

This philosophy is further elaborated in Articles Three and Four, without reference to rights:

"Art. 3. The State will motivate natural and juridical persons as well as collectives to protect nature; it will promote respect towards all the elements that form an ecosystem.

"Art. 4. The State will apply precaution and restriction measures in all the activities that can lead to the extinction of species, the destruction of the ecosystems or the permanent alteration of the natural cycles."

It may sound strange to say that Nature or Pachamama has a right to exist, but there is a logic to this if the working languages and culture of its drafters were Spanish and English.

What the Constitution is expressing is the necessity of recognizing the legitimacy and integrity of, and showing respect for, the realm "where life is reproduced and exists" and allowing, that is, not violating, its persistence and regeneration through its own vital cycles and structures.

Assertion of the right of nature "to exist, persist, maintain and regenerate its vital cycles, structure, functions and its processes in evolution" is also a carefully worded negation of the culture of genetic engineering, with its deliberate and systematic violation of the integrity of an organism and its disruption of the organism's (plant or animal) maintenance of its vital cycles and processes. Thus Article Four follows logically: "The introduction of organisms and organic and inorganic material that can alter in a definitive way the national genetic patrimony is prohibited."

The is a radically different expression of the similar view articulated in the Genetic Bill of Rights discussed earlier.

While we may rejoice in the philosophy expressed in the new Ecuadorean constitution, it was only a very short time before legislation was introduced in the National Assembly that opened the door to mining in the well-organized Indigenous Amazonian regions of the country. Under strong pressure from President Correa, the Legislative Commission approved a new mining law on Jan. 12, 2009, that many believe violates the Constitution.[107]

While it is refreshing (and logical) that a strong Indigenous cosmovision is expressed in the new constitution of Ecuador, it is more surprising to find a similar consciousness being expressed in a conservative European country such as Switzerland (while recognizing that it is, after all, the home of Rudolf Steiner and biodynamic farming).

In the 1990s, the Swiss constitution was amended in order to defend the dignity of all creatures, including plants, against unwanted consequences of genetic manipulation. When the amendment was turned into a law – known as the Gene Technology Act – it didn't say anything specific about plants. But in 2008 the Swiss Parliament asked a panel of philosophers, lawyers, geneticists and theologians to establish the meaning of flora's dignity. In April, 2008, the team published a 22-page treatise on "the moral consideration of plants for their own sake". Defenders of the law argue that it "reflects a broader, progressive effort to protect the sanctity of living things"[108] – again without reference to rights.

Following this, at the time the new Ecuadorean constitution was being voted on, the Rheinauer Theses on the Rights of Plants[109] was put forth by a group of Swiss scientists, farmers and others (as mentioned earlier). Acknowledging in the introduction "that all living organisms have a common origin" and that "plants will in the final analysis always remain a mystery to us", they propose the theses "with the aim of allowing plants to express themselves for their own sake and claiming rights on their behalf". They then elaborate 29 theses on the life of plants, followed by six "rights of plants", drawn from these theses.

Among the 29 theses, which are clearly harmonious with the opening articles of the new Ecuadorian constitution, are the following:

"Like all living beings, plants react to their constantly changing environments. They communicate with each other and with other life forms.... Plants experience the world in their own way. They have a life of their own .... To view plants as entirely disposable objects is to do them an injustice.... If we perceive plants as machines, this reveals something about ourselves, the observers, not about the plant's nature. This mechanistic view extends itself to all living beings – also to humans...."

The authors then introduce the six "rights of plants", saying,

"If we accord rights to plants, this does not mean that we should not eat them or use them in other ways anymore. Just as according rights to animals does not mean excluding them from the food chain. It means much more that we respect the uniqueness of plants and acknowledge limits in our dealings with them."

The six rights which they attribute to plants are: "reproductive rights, right to independence, right to evolution, right to survival as a species, right to respectful research and development and right not to be patented." These rights, they point out, "have been formulated by humans. They therefore have validity only to the extent that they can be observed or contravened by human action." They might have added, 'and understood by Europeans'.

The last sentence of the introduction to the theses ("with the aim of allowing plants to express themselves for their own sake and claiming rights on their behalf") introduces a contradiction: the 29 theses, proposed "with the aim of allowing plants to express themselves for their own sake," is straightforward, but the human attitude toward and relationship with plants implied in the theses is distorted by then speaking about "claiming rights on their behalf", which elevates humans over plants. I wish the authors of the theses had said, instead, "we express our willingness to practice and advocate respect for plants and their integrity".*

---

* In explaining the language of the Rheinauer Theses, the prime mover behind the statement, Florianne Koechlin, told me that in Switzerland there had been big discussions around animal rights and the idea that 'animals are not things'. Now, after years of controversy, there are (at least in Switzerland) laws for species-specific treatment of farm animals. This goes along with the general, slowly growing acceptance that animals have needs and cannot be treated as machines; are not things; that they have a dignity on their own which means they have the right

(continued...)

However, we do not live in a perfect word, and the Rheinauer Theses, like the Constitution of Ecuador, express a vastly more generous view of the world and our limited place in it than the materialist, controlling attitude (such as that driving genetic engineering) that characterizes far too much of western culture.

As I have said before, rights is a juridical concept, while respect is a moral concept. Respect requires taking responsibility, whereas under rights, responsibility becomes legally defined and shuffled off to the state.

Clearly we face a major obstacle is trying to think about how to live in a universe in which we humans are not at the centre and are not the focus and primary beneficiary (however short-term) of all Creation.*

---

*(...continued)
to being well cared for. This 'rights-discussion' brought the issue 'animals are not things' right into the whole society. "I'm a political animal," she wrote, "and for me/us it's important to have tools like the rights discussion – the 'dignity-of-creature-has-to-be respected' article – in our constitution."

* I try to use the term Creation for what is more usually referred to in 'objective' terms as Nature. This is because I object to the implication that Nature is out there while we are in here, in command. Creation, to my mind, implies something greater and more awesome than Nature. In western thinking, nature has been so reduced – by rationalist thinking and reductionist science – to a shopping cart or rail car full of 'resources' that the concept has lost all non-utilitarian meaning.

HOLDING AND WITHHOLDING:
RIGHTS OF INTELLECT

The social construction of 'intellectual property' and the ownership 'rights' accompanying it has an interesting history, and like all history, a lot depends on who is telling the story. Unfortunately, the only story most people hear is that told by the World Trade Organization (WTO), the promoters of the TRIPS agreement (Trade-Related aspects of Intellectual Property Rights)* and neoliberals in general. Deliberately or instinctively, their way of telling the story rests on and advances the idea that rights in intellectual property are

---

* TRIPS: Agreement on Trade-related Aspects of Intellectual Property Rights: administered by the World Trade Organization (WTO), sets down minimum standards for many forms of intellectual property (IP) regulation, negotiated at the end of the Uruguay Round of the General Agreement on Tariffs and Trade (GATT) in 1994. From the preamble: "Desiring to reduce distortions and impediments to international trade, and taking into account the need to promote effective and adequate protection of intellectual property rights, and to ensure that measures and procedures to enforce intellectual property rights do not themselves become barriers to legitimate trade ..."

universally recognized and 'natural', like the assumption expressed in the Universal Declaration of Human Rights.

Since the 18th century, in the world of capitalism and enlightenment, the product of that aspect of a person identified as the intellect has been granted rights in the 'property' emanating from it.[110] These rights are widely known, in Western cultures at least, as intellectual property rights, and like human rights, their coverage has advanced in wondrous ways. Intellectual property rights (IPRs), in the form of patents and trademarks as well as copyright, are now applied to everything from seeds and genetic elements to mechanical gadgets, paintings, labels and logos, computer software and, of course, the written word, where it all started.

Patents, although their application has been greatly extended, have historically been applied to material objects of invention: a mousetrap could be patented as a novel product of invention, with the inventive (novel) step identified as such. It is the patent on the mousetrap, not the mousetrap itself, that constitutes intellectual property. The basic rule of intellectual property, at least historically, is that an idea is not property and cannot be owned, but the expression of it can. This means it has to take, or be given, a material, communicable form in order to be owned.

A major expansion of what could be considered intellectual property came in 1980 when the US Supreme Court ruled, in the Chakrabarty case, that a genetically engineered oil-eating microbe was not a product of nature but Chakrabarty's invention.*[111] The scope of what could be considered intellectual property and thus patented increased eight years later when the US Patent and Trademark Office issued the first patent on a living animal, a transgenic mouse

---

* Ananda Chakrabarty was a microbiologist working for General Electric when he 'invented' his oil-eating microbe. Chakrabarty himself admitted that he invented nothing, he "simply shuffled genes, changing bacteria that already existed."[110]

engineered to contain various alien genetic sequences making it prone to cancer for use in drug development. There are now thousands upon thousands of patents worldwide on various forms of living organisms and their components.

This profound change in what is considered legally patentable required a rule change at the patent office as well. Since in many cases the inventor cannot fully describe his biological invention – because he does not really know, and cannot know, just what the object of the patent application actually does or how it works because biology is too complex and unpredictable – the patent offices now allow samples of the object of the patent to be deposited in lieu of a full description.

Trademark is the third form of what is called intellectual property. A trademark is a device of identity. The product it applies to may not be either copyrighted or patented, but the logo and label design can be registered as trademarks and become, thereby, intellectual property, indicated by its accompanying © or ™.

What each of these forms of intellectual property grant to their owners is the right of exclusion and, in a market economy, exclusion creates scarcity, which inflates commercial value.

With every intellectual property right granted by the state there are two 'products': the object of the patent/copyright/trademark and the intellectual property right that goes with it. These intellectual properties may then become autonomous properties, commodities bought and sold as such. In each case the value of the intellectual property lies in its legal recognition by the state, which makes intellectual property rights eerily similar to human rights.

Actually, the rights ascribed to intellectual property (a term that first appeared in 1845 according to the Oxford English Dictionary) bear little resemblance to human rights and the other forms of rights claims that have been discussed so far. In fact, it has been seriously suggested that it is time to change the language of IP: "The privilege that lies at the heart of all intellectual property is a state-based, rule governed privilege to interfere in the negative liberties of others. If this is so, then the language of property rights should be replaced by the term, 'intellectually-based monopoly privileges'."[112]

Contemporary promoters of IPRs, including the WTO and the TRIPS agreement, as I said earlier, assume and claim that IPRs are natural and universal. However, Christopher May argues convincingly that, "Although the institution of intellectual property has become ... increasingly globalized (indeed it has potentially been universalized), it owes its origins to the particular circumstances and history of European capitalism from the late fifteenth century in Venice onwards. This is to stress that there is nothing 'natural' about intellectual property rights; rather they represent the consolidation of specific commercial interests in capital accumulation."[113] May also stresses that the commercial interest in IPRs is directly linked to and dependent on state regulation and the enforcement powers of the state.

According to historian Carla Hesse, the rise of intellectual property as we know it can be traced back to the creation of the title of King's Printer in 1504. This position gave the appointee the exclusive right to print royal proclamations, statutes, and other official documents. By 1557 the English crown had reorganized the guild of printers and publishers, known as the Stationers' Company, and given it a virtual monopoly over printing and publishing.[114]

Without recording devices and various forms of reproduction and translation, the spoken word or visual image could not be replicated except by hand. Multiple prints of text or artwork could be made from a single block or a plate, but neither the plate nor the prints themselves could be reproduced. The printing press (attributed to Gutenberg, 1439) was the only means of reproducing the expression of an idea in any commercial way, and this was slow and expensive – or at least a very far cry from digital reproduction today – though it did allow the development of a middle-class reading public and a dramatic expansion of literary piracy to challenge the market monopoly held by the guilds.* At the same time, authors were coming to view themselves as the originators and thus owners of their own work, and rather than selling a material manuscript (i.e., actual words on real paper, or parchment) to a publisher, they increasingly sought simply to sell the 'rights' to a single edition.

In other words, what in time came to be the moral claim or entitlement known as copyright (literally, the exclusive right to copy) began life as a monopoly privilege granted by the sovereign, i.e. the state. That privilege was curbed in England in 1709 with the Statute of Anne which ruled that authors, and those who had purchased a manuscript from an author, would have an exclusive right to publish the work for only fourteen years.

The actual idea of intellectual property only emerged with a changing attitude toward knowledge, as Carla Hesse describes:

"The concept of intellectual property – the idea that an idea can be owned – is a child of the European Enlightenment. It was only when people began to believe that knowledge came from the human mind working upon the senses – rather than through divine revelation, assisted by the study of ancient texts – that it became possible to imagine humans as creators, and

---

* From the invention of the printing press it was more or less three hundred years to the next technological step to lithography (1796), a little more than another century to the offset press (1903) and something like half a century more to photocopiers and the throw-away reproduction technologies of today.

hence owners, of new ideas rather than as mere transmitters of eternal verities."[115]

The various forms of intellectual property have limited lifespans and along with a continuing pressure to expand the scope of copyrights and patents there is relentless pressure from the corporate rights holders to extend their terms. The term of copyright is now the life of the author plus 50 years in most countries, and for patents it is 20 years from the date of filing of the patent application.

The argument behind both the exclusive right and the limitation of this right is that society benefits from the work of writers, artists and inventors and therefore the public ought to provide incentives for their creativity (or what is now in the patent realm referred to as 'innovation'). At the same time, the public interest in access to the 'protected' work, for purposes of elaboration or further invention, should limit the claims of private ownership. Unfortunately, and contrary to the intent of copyrights and patents in the first place, the owners of property have steadily gained the upper hand, and the terms of protection of their 'private property' have been steadily advanced at the expense of public access. How copyright can be an incentive to creativity for 50 years after the author's death is a question we will come to shortly.

While printing presses were becoming a significant means of production and reproduction, and authors were claiming their literary works as their own creations, John Locke was busy laying the philosophical groundwork for the hallowing of property and the conjoining of two historic streams of European history: the development of the idea that a person's very being was expressed in the work of his hands over which, as a result, he could claim ownership and the rights of property; and the development of the idea that a person's ideas were similarly his own, and his own property, as emanations of his being and labour. There was no longer any basis for claiming that some things could not be considered property and could not be owned, at least within the culture of capitalism.*

Carys Craig describes succinctly the foundation of the cultural power of copyright: "The property right conferred by copyright legislation is understood as a reward for intellectual labour and effort, and that reward is in turn regarded as something 'deserved'. What is deserved becomes an entitlement."[116] What began as a matter of social policy to provide an incentive (and reward) to authors grew into an individual legal right. "Natural law has a powerful normative and legitimizing force which comes into play at the moment when copyright is recast in individualistic, rights-based terms. The inevitable result is the widening of copyright protection and the concomitant undermining of the public interest."[117]

Over time, not only has the scope and duration of copyright been extended, but its initial rationale of providing an incentive to writers has been turned into an income stream for rights holders who are now predominantly major media corporations. While the publication information page of a book will identify the publisher and attribute copyright to the author, this may well be misleading in that the rights of the copyright may be assigned to the publisher. In the case of newspapers, magazines and other mass media, it is frequently, if not usually, the publisher that holds copyright and can do what it wants with the author's intellectual 'product', be it written, audio or design, thus restoring, in effect, the monopoly of the guilds. The author-creator

---

* As Allison Hudgins told me: "I think there are many writers who have not thought much past the pain it took to produce the final product, which generates an awfully powerful ownership sense. Which may be comparable, in a sense, to giving birth to an infant. Hard work, rightly called labour. But is the mother a labourer or the owner of a product?"

becomes a contract employee and the intellect has been reduced to a marketable property.[118]

This is no accident. As Christopher May and Susan Sell describe it:

"Over its history, property has moved from a common understanding as physical things held for the owner's use to the more modern conception of property as assets that can be used or otherwise sold to another potential user ... This move from holding to withholding, the ability to restrict use, is crucially important for our history of intellectual property."[119]

May and Sell elaborate on a crucial characteristic of "the institution of property in knowledge": the construction of scarcity where it does not necessarily exist. "Scarcity needs to be constructed because knowledge, unlike physical property, generally is not rivalrous. In a capitalist economy the construction of rivalrousness is the central role of intellectual property." They point out that "when knowledge or information is to be the subject of legal rules that construct scarcity, nonlegal justifications are deployed, often taking the form of ideas about reward for effort or the 'efficient' use of knowledge resources."[120]

In other words, the idea of intellectual property, and rights thereto, is considerably less altruistic and more pernicious than many authors, 'rights holders' and lawyers would like to admit, or than the public believes.

This situation has now created yet another set of rights, called 'user rights', which transforms the public into a function of the market identified as users and attempts to construct a counter claim to that of IPR holders. It's a never-ending downward spiral in the name of achieving 'balance' between owners and users.* The needs of society – the public

---

* In Canada, 'copyright reform', as it is referred to by its Conservative Party sponsors and media lobbyists, is all about balance, that is,

(continued...)

– do not enter the picture, even though, as May and Sell put it, "The common use of information and knowledge across society is one of the key elements of a shared social existence."[121]

A "shared social existence" is clearly the concern of corporate copyright holders only insofar as they can create a cultural climate that is commercially rewarding for them. This means a shared social existence created by and dependent upon, if not addicted to, the commercial creations designed to induce this dependency and its consequent corporate profits.* This is exactly what we see with the ubiquity of the personal listening device – with the prefix 'i' as an expression of the individualism of the whole project – and the high-stake battles over various forms of rights. This is a long way from nurturing a shared social existence based on freely shared cultural history, shared knowledge and open access to information, although there are aspects of filesharing, social networking, and internet tools such as 'wikis' that are, consciously or not, running counter to these intellectual enclosures.

Efforts to first gain legal recognition for the workings of the mind and intellect as property; then to claim private ownership over, and hence rights to, ideas and their expression and replication; and thus to create scarcity and market value, have a far longer history than that of rights in seeds, but the similarity of intents and processes is striking. In both cases, the essential issue is the same: do ideas, any more than seeds, emerge *ex nihilo* at the hands of plant breeders or

---

*(...continued)
balancing the interests of copyright holders/owners and users of copyright material. There is no place for the public, and the corporate rights holders far outweigh individual users when it comes to lobbying for legislation.

* Walt Disney and his commercial heirs can probably be credited with initiating this socially destructive commercial enterprise.

writers solely as a product of their labour? The answer is obviously, no. Writers, artists, musicians – all creators, in fact – build on the work of others before them and around them – whether it is generations of farmers who have selected and saved seeds, or the authors who have built upon the ideas of artists before them out of un-owned material in the public domain.

The claim of exclusive rights is anathema to creativity. The claim that it is only by means of copyright, and other mechanisms designed to create scarcity, that writers, artists and musicians can make a living from their work is an ideological assertion. The real question is, if society values the work of its artisans, musicians and cultural workers, how are these people to be compensated so that they can carry on with their contributions to the public good? One of Canada's answers to this question is the Canada Council for the Arts, created by the federal government in 1957 to foster and promote the study and enjoyment of, and the production of works in the arts by providing grants and services to professional Canadian artists and arts organizations. Another is the Social Sciences and Humanities Research Council (SSHRC), created by an act of Canadian Parliament in 1977, which promotes and supports university-based research and training in the humanities and social sciences. The scope of the SSHRC has been severely limited by the current Conservative Federal Government and in its March 2009 budget it dictated that SSHRC funding was to go only to research that is "focused on business-related degrees".

I have to acknowledge a self-interest in this question as I know from experience that few authors actually make a living from their writing, pretenses notwithstanding, and without significant support from a short-lived program of grants to "independent scholars" of the Social Sciences and Humanities Research Council I don't think I would have found either the means or encouragement to have written two of my earlier books.

The "the institution of property in knowledge" and with it the construction of IPRs can be likened to the enclosures of village commons in Britain in the 19th century and earlier. The fencing off of the commons for the benefit of the feudal lords and resulting exclusion of peasants deprived them of their independent existence and contributed to the creation of a labour force for the Industrial Revolution. What has been described as the enclosure of the mind and its dedication to corporate interests and big-name heavily promoted writers and musicians has, fortunately, generated a counter movement that recognizes that artists, writers, seed breeders, musicians and inventors all build on the work of those who have gone before. Unfortunately, even Creative Commons licenses, the GPL (General Public License) and others, still, ultimately, rest on the assumption that ideas can be property. They simply want to liberalize copyright to a greater or lesser extent for public ('user') and creator benefit in order to restore some balance to the copyright regime, now heavily weighted in favour of commercial rights holders. While this may be a step in the direction of intellectual freedom, it does not challenge the underlying assumption that private property is sacred.

Copyright could have a positive role in ensuring that originals remain intact so that they can continue to inspire. Copyright might also be one of a number of means to compensate cultural workers for their labour. But they should not be seen as a way to limit the interpretation, derivation or any other uses of the basic material. Copyright needs to be a form of recognition and registry, not of corporate profit and control.

RIGHT TO DIE
A DEATH OF ONE'S OWN

"Who cares anything today for a finely-finished death?
No one. Even the rich, who could after all afford this
luxury of dying in full detail, are beginning to be
careless and indifferent; the wish to have a death of
one's own is growing ever rarer. A while yet and it will
be just as rare as a life of one's own. Heavens, it's all
there. One arrives, one finds a life, ready made, one
has only to put it on. One wants to leave or one is
compelled to: anyway, no effort: *Voilà votre mort,
monsieur.*" – Rainer Maria Rilke[122]

It's odd that the right to life ranks high on our list of 'goods'
while the right to die is, in most jurisdictions, illegal, if not
anathema, at least in the enlightened culture of the west. So
abortion rights are opposed by the advocates of the right to
life. Both camps wind up treating life as a principle, not a
living organism or a person.[123]

Both the emotion-laden slogan of 'right to life' and
the equally emotion-laden notion of 'right to die' are singularly individualistic, in keeping with rights generally, and

both are at home in a culture that has made a fetish of life.* What I mean by 'making a fetish of life' is that the real person is subsumed to the apparently more highly regarded 'life'. 'Saving lives' then becomes a powerful mantra, opening the door to the business interests of prolonging life: the pharmaceutical industry that steadily escalates the number of ailments** that are reclassified as diseases to be treated with their most profitable drugs; technology manufacturers and marketers that continually push their ever more costly machines to 'save lives'; and now genetic interventions that are intended to save the lives of the unborn of future generations from supposedly heritable diseases.

"Medicine has become very good at eliminating acute causes of death such as infections, but the downside of this success is that people live long enough to suffer from degenerative disease. What's more, many acute forms of death have been converted to chronic ill health or disability. Heart attack has become heart failure; stroke has become vascular dementia. Diabetes, AIDS and even some cancers have been converted from acute causes of death to chronic disabilities. Another unfortunate factor is that it is much more profitable for pharmaceutical companies to develop drugs that keep patients alive but uncured, rather than curing the disease which loses the customer. The situation is not helped by the charities and funding agencies that focus on preventing death rather than disease or ageing.... Hospices ought to be as ubiquitous and well-funded as maternity hospitals.... Death is not the enemy; it is an integral part of life."[124]

---

* The term was articulated in 1989 by Ivan Illich in a talk entitled 'The Institutional Construction of a New Fetish: Human Life'

** The Nelson Canadian Dictionary defines "ailment" as "a physical or mental disorder". You are not likely to get a prescription for a disorder.

If we were to think in the old fashioned, rather indeterminate, terms of 'ailment' and 'illness', then we might be better prepared to think about providing the healthy environment and working conditions that would greatly reduce illness, disease and disability – and the costs thereof – in the first place. The fetishization of life, however, allows Life to become a marketing tool, whether it is in an ad for some industry-sponsored patient advocacy group or for some new miracle drug. As Ivan Illich succinctly put it, "A Life is amenable to management, to improvement and to evaluation in terms of available resources in a way which is unthinkable when we speak of a person."

There is, to be sure, a growing recognition that the drive to save a life must be tempered by consideration of the quality of life facing the one saved and for those caring for that person. Quality, however, is a highly subjective judgement compared to the question of whether a person is dead or alive, though increasingly heroic efforts to save and extend lives can create doubt about whether a person is actually alive or really dead.

Having turned individual lives into objects to be preserved, we can become blind to the killing conditions of systemic deprivation and hunger, environmental destruction and war itself – whether it is the 'war on terror', the attempt to eliminate Palestine,[125] the genocide of big dam construction in India or the Amazon or the consequences of mining activities. Instead we can talk about 'human rights abuses' and the 'fight for rights', with the result that the rights discourse exercises a kind of tyranny over us, blinding us to the larger underlying structural issues that must be addressed.

In this larger context, it is not surprising that the right to die is put forward in the same way as the right to life. These both follow from the legal construction of rights and become legal battles employing large numbers of lawyers. The actual persons involved are replaced by their avatars[126]

and become more or less sponsors of the battle over their
life.*[127]

Under the rights regime, no one is free to come and
go as they please, or as they 'choose' in the neoliberal par-
lance of consumer choice. We must each take responsibility

---

* "If I cannot give consent to my own death, then whose body is this?
Who owns my life?" – Sue Rodriguez, Globe & Mail, 23/11/93.

"Sue Rodriguez was diagnosed with the terminal disease ALS in
1991. After coming to terms with the fact that ALS will reduce her to
a drooling, paralysed shell of her former self, Sue Rodriguez decided to
kill herself while life was still good, but after making that personal
decision, she ran into a legal roadblock: assisted suicide and euthanasia
are against the law in Canada, and anyone who aids a person in
committing suicide can be jailed for up to 14 years. Suicide, by contrast,
is legal. But since Rodriguez would be physically incapable of killing
herself due to the nature of her disease, she would need assistance,
thereby breaking the law.

"Rodriguez felt she had a right to die with the help of a doctor at a
time of her choosing, but she didn't want to break the law. She took her
case to the B.C. Supreme Court, arguing that section 241(b) of
Canada's Criminal code violated her rights guaranteed under the
Canadian Charter of Rights and Freedoms and that she has the
constitutional right to control her body.

"In November 1992 a parliamentary committee in Ottawa was in
the midst of 'recodifying' the Criminal Code, including the sections on
euthanasia and assisted suicide, but since Rodriguez was already too
weak to travel to Ottawa she addressed the committee via videotape.
'Who owns my life?, Whose body is this?' she asked.

"After losing in both the B.C. Supreme Court and the B.C. Court
of Appeal, Sue Rodriguez took her case to the Supreme Court of Canada
asking it to grant her the right to assisted suicide.

"On Sept. 29, 1993, the Supreme Court judges ruled against
Rodriguez in a split 5-4 decision. In writing the majority judgement,
Justice John Sopinka expressed the 'deepest sympathy' for Rodriguez,
but ultimately ruled that she cannot be exempt from the law. 'No
consensuses can be found in favour of the decriminalization of assisted
suicide. To the extent that there is a consensus, it is that human life
must be respected.'

"In the end Sue Rodriguez defied the law by choosing the time and
the method of her death, Feb. 12, 1994." – CBC archives.[126]

for our life, we are told, while we are increasingly bombarded with warnings about this or that risk. (Look at the warnings on any electrical appliance or visit a toy store and look at the plethora of tags on the toys and infant equipment.) And thus we must make every effort not only to keep alive every individual foetus and premature infant, no matter at what immediate or long-term cost – emotional, social and financial – but also to prolong life, no matter how degrading and costly.

"When Bruce Hardy's kidney cancer spread to his lung, his doctor recommended an expensive new pill from Pfizer. But Mr. Hardy is British, and the British health authorities refused to buy the medicine. A clinical trial showed that the pill, called Sutent, delays cancer progression for six months at an estimated treatment cost of $54,000. But at that price, Mr. Hardy's life is not worth prolonging, according to a British government agency, the National Institute for Health and Clinical Excellence. The institute ... has decided that Britain, except in rare cases, can afford only $22,750, to save six months of a citizen's life."[128]

We are all going to die of something, with something, by something.

"I have long suspected that heart disease is 'the leading cause of death' because it is categorically impossible to die of old age. Thus spurious facticity meets disease mongering *et puis voilà* pharma finds an epidemic."[129]

And the attending physician has to write something as the cause of death on the death certificate:

"According to the US Center for Disease Control (CDC), the leading causes of death among those ages 65 and over are, in descending order, heart disease, cancer, stroke, respiratory disease, Alzheimer's disease, diabetes, influenza, kidney disease, accidents and infection. Maybe so. But that's because people are not allowed to die of old age – at least old age cannot be listed as the cause of death on the official documents ... Neither should 'infirmity' or 'senescence' appear as a cause of death, according to the CDC handbook on how to fill out a death certificate.... Instead, every death must be attributed to a single disease, which is the immediate cause of death. A second disease may be cited as the intermediate cause, and a third as the underlying condition.... But 80- and 90-year-olds don't usually die of one thing. Little by little, the wheels fall off the bicycle.... Eventually, as with all machines, the human body simply wears out.... And what would it mean for public policy if the leading cause of death among the very old was 'wheels falling off bicycle'? Would long-term care, its costs and indignities, find a place on the national agenda?"[130]

One could reasonably expect a culture that claims to honour and respect human rights to even more strongly respect the person and their life and death, and to give death its due honour and allow it to unfold without violent interventions and heroic measures to thwart it. In such a culture the 'right to die' would have no place.

This would hold as true at the beginning of life as at the end. A 'right to life' would not lead to the attempt to save – or salvage – every conceived infant, no matter how premature, but would give way to a recognition that the heroic measures taken to birth and keep alive an infant that could not possibly survive otherwise are just that: measures taken to make heroes out of doctors and medical technology. They are not respectful of either life or death. Just because it can be done is no reason that it should be done. (Which, of course, applies widely, including genetic engineering.)[131]

One of the hardest lessons we had to learn when we were sheep farming was to recognize that when a mother abandoned a new-born lamb, she probably knew

something we did not. Our heroic measures to save every
lamb usually turned out to be in vain. Either the lamb
would die as soon as we took it out of intensive care, or it
might live to grow into a runt and then drop dead. We
had to accept that the time we were devoting to saving
every lamb was time that would have been better spent
caring for the rest of the flock.

There is a finality about the death of a nice, tidy,
isolated dot* that leaves nothing behind, except perhaps
some property. The death of a person living in a complex
social web is very different.

"To see injustice in the world was not bearable for
Jake. He was a man who had to speak his truth. He
was a man who strived to live by his ideals.... Over the
years his advancing age brought him a state of peace
and equanimity, which he carried with him through
his final days. His preparing to leave this world was a
beautiful time, surrounded by family, at home. He
accepted his life, was grateful for its many gifts and was
then ready to let it go.... As his body weakened, his
spirit grew stronger. He had used himself up completely, given all that he had and is now ready to move
on in spirit...."[132]

Jake may have used himself up, but the bits of himself
he left on deposit, one might say, with a variety of people,
will continue to enrich the tangle of relationships that
constitute the fabric of society. The death of a dot may be
quite final, but the death of a complex organism is a continuing process.

---

* With reference to my 'dots, lots of dots' diagram, p.28

THE RIGHT TO INTERVENE

When I started thinking seriously about the language and concept of rights, I had no idea that I would have to include the 'right to intervene', or what is now sometimes referred to as Responsibility to Protect (R2P) with its more humanitarian overtones.

When Médecins sans Frontières was founded in 1971, 'without borders' sounded clean and altruistic, not limited by petty nationalist claims of sovereignty with their traditional 'rights to exclude'. The implications of 'without borders' for sovereignty, international law and peace were not the subject of discussion with our progressive friends. We hardly gave a thought to the implications of over-riding the national boundaries and state sovereignty that were understood to be the basis of post World War II stability and political order (whatever we might have thought of that order at the time). Our opposition to the dictatorships in Central and South America meant calling for withdrawal of political support of the murderous dictatorships and commercial support through investment and trade, not military intervention by the US or anyone else.

However, the internal revolt (or civil war, depending on your perspective) in Nigeria in the late 1960s and the dramatic appeals for public funding of humanitarian aid to feed the starving infants with swollen bellies in the secessionist state that took the name of Biafra changed all that. The contentious issue of intervention into supposedly sovereign states has, since then, become an important challenge to international peace and justice. And this is without even beginning to talk about the military interventions in Afghanistan and Iraq in the name of human rights and humanitarian aid.

Disgraced former US President George W. Bush gave us a wake-up call – which we have not adequately heeded – when, at the start of military operations against Afghanistan, he announced that "as we strike military targets, we will also drop food, medicine and supplies to the starving men and women and children of Afghanistan."[133]

"Back in 1990," David Chandler wrote in 2002, "few people would have imagined that, within the decade, the international human rights community would be advocating the military occupation of independent countries on human rights grounds, the establishment of long-term protectorates, or the bombing of major European cities on a humanitarian basis... The shift from needs-based to rights-based aid provision has paved the way for today's conception of 'humanitarian militarism'."[134]

'Humanitarian militarism' is a harsh term, but the military actions carried out in Afghanistan, Iraq, the former Yugoslavia and most recently Gaza were far more than police actions or measures taken to bring or restore justice to 'rogue states' and unpleasant dictatorships.

Pierre Micheletti, president of Médecins du Monde, ascribes the emergence of the concept of humanitarian aid to the war in Nigeria, which "in just 33 combat months, left hundreds of thousands dead (mostly from starvation and sickness) and three million refugees."[135]

"The Biafran war was the crucible in which the modern humanitarian aid movement was forged. From May 1967 to January 1970 the Nigerian Federal Military Government fought the Ibos who had established the Republic of Biafra in the east of the country. During this civil war, challenging and disturbing international networks emerged, as did militant aid workers who, for the first time, used public opinion to influence foreign policy.... Political and ethnic struggles obscured economic objectives for the war: Biafra held 80% of Nigeria's oil reserves .... That's why major international powers and multinational oil companies were so soon interested in this civil war.... It was in the context of this war, and its new media visibility, that a group of young French doctors described the events and mobilised public opinion and governments to support the Biafrans. Médecins sans Frontières (MSF) was born, followed by Médecins du Monde (MDM).... So the origins of the humanitarian movement are ambiguous."[136]

To describe as 'ambiguous' the motivation behind international intervention in a secessionist province of a sovereign state – where ethnic conflict masks the underlying issues of oil reserves and tribal rivalries – is clearly a generous understatement.

The actual formulation of 'duty to intervene' did not occur until 1989 at a conference on law and humanitarian morality given by Bernard Kouchner, a founder of Médecins sans Frontières and now French foreign minister, and law professor Mario Bettati. "The right to intervene," however, "without any basis in law, remains a vague concept for those who might have recourse to it – states, international organizations and NGOs."[137]

While a doctrine of the right to intervene on an international or global scale has only recently been elaborated, intervention in the affairs of others in the name of human rights has been going on for some time, as discussed earlier in connection with the right to life and the right to die. Now, however, not only is a right to intervene claimed, but also a responsibility and even duty to intervene at the beginning as well as the end of human lives. There are legal and moral claims for the rights of the foetus, or even an embryo, entailing intervention with no possibility of consent. The life being intervened in is physically incapable of exercising any attributed rights: it remains an object of manipulation by alien intervenors. Yet it is the victim – the object of the rights claims – that suffers the effects. Those seeking to 'save' the life of a malformed foetus or a toxified embryo are not likely to also campaign for adequate public responsibility to care for the consequent individual. Their 'right to life' does not necessarily include parental assistance, special education, and so on for the life of the person. To be morally valid, the 'right to life' campaigners must advocate equally strongly for public support for those responsible for the person. They should also be pacifists. With right to life must come responsibility – and respect – for all lives.

Similar situations arise at the end of life, whenever that might occur, as we saw in the preceding chapter. Those claiming the right – and responsibility, on moral grounds – to intervene to prolong a life do not necessarily bear the consequences of that intervention. They may have no legal responsibility to care for the surviving person and do not bear the attendant pain or suffering.

Assertion of the right to intervene carries with it the same moral questions on the international level as on the directly personal level. Intervention must entail long-term engagement and responsibility. It also demands careful consideration of the historical development of the current situation, particularly its colonial and commercial history, and the possible political consequences of any intervention.

Take, for example, the form of intervention referred to as investments ('direct foreign investments' in technical terms) that are viewed as essential to economic development by capitalist economists and governments. These interventions, carried out by private corporations in pursuit of wealth by extracting and exporting natural elements such as minerals and oil, often involve significant abuse and exploitation of people as well as ecological destruction. Not even in the name of development can these interventions be rationalized as humanitarian; nor can the corporate global search for cheap labour with its attendant consequences of abuse and exploitation and the use of private militias to protect corporate claims.

Generally, however, intervention has come to be understood as the moral responsibility (or duty) to intervene anywhere in the world to deliver humanitarian aid or to attempt to halt abuse and violation of human beings. Bernard Kouchner articulated this position when he wrote, in 1999, that "we need to establish a forward-looking right of the world community to actively intervene in the affairs of sovereign nations to prevent an explosion of human rights violations.... Now it is necessary to take the further step of using the right to intervention as a preventative measure to stop wars before they start and to stop murderers before they kill."[138] Kouchner does not define who or what constitutes the 'world community', nor does he discuss the implications of political alignment, such as his own, even though interventions do not necessarily produce the outcomes desired by the intervenors, and may, in fact, make matters worse for those the intervention is supposed to aid.*[139]

---

* "It is Kouchner, more than anyone, who has eroded the distinction between philanthropy and combat," writes Christopher Caldwell.

(continued...)

For James Orbinski, a front-line MSF doctor, administrator, and MSF past-president, on the other hand, the struggle to understand the "difference and relationship between humanitarian and political responsibilities" is constant. After Orbinski accepted the Nobel Peace Prize on behalf of MSF in 1999, he was invited to address the UN Security Council in New York. He writes that he emphasized "the necessity of a political response to political problems, a humanitarian response to humanitarian problems, and for robust and credible peacekeeping forces for security and protection concerns." On the ground, in Somalia, Kosovo, or Rwanda, as Orbinski's deeply moving account of his experiences make clear, there is no simple clear answer to what is humanitarian and what is political and what is required, and possibly no answer at all. "I referred to Rwanda, about which no member of the Security Council had been able to use the word *genocide*, and where the political crime of genocide erased the possibility of humanitarianism. The Security Council authorized a humanitarian intervention as a solution – one that obscured or sanitized the problem, and thus erased the UN's political responsibility to intervene to stop genocide."[140]

Human rights violations are seldom enumerated or the abuses described, just as the genocide in Rwanda and neighbouring territories was not to be described as such by the UN. The term may refer to driving peasants off their land to make way for industrial agriculture, assassination of union organizers, systematic rape, imprisonment and torture, and mass killing and genocide. As I said earlier, the terms 'human rights abuses' or 'human rights violations' are, apparently,

---

*(...continued)
"Kouchner's great achievement at the time [1988] was to theorize... the right to disregard national sovereignty and intervene in countries experiencing humanitarian crises – and to get it codified, in UN Resolution 43/131."[138]

presumed to carry sufficient moral weight that we don't need to know to what they actually refer. Nor are we encouraged to think about the concept of rights itself or of the ways in which it is being used. We are certainly not encouraged to think in structural terms, that is, about the political and economic structures of society that create, harbour or encourage injustice and violence, such as extreme economic inequity and discrimination of all sorts. The hiring of mercenaries to protect their 'interests' is not a subject one finds discussed in the business press along with how the mining and oil industry stocks are faring in the market, regardless of the social and ecological consequences of their business activities. Nor are the social consequences of intervention – humanitarian, commercial or military – in a politically-charged situation.

The right to intervene is, like rights previously described, essentially individualistic in that it is directed to and for the sake of individuals, albeit a mass of individuals, such as the food programs and medical aid.*[141] This is not a bad thing, but it should not be confused with building an egalitarian society. Humanitarian aid may well, in fact, deliberately and effectively bypass the state and its agencies, corrupt or not. Humanitarian aid, like intervention to address 'human rights abuses', may actually be aligned with national and corporate interests in access to oil (Biafra is an unfortunate example, Iraq another) or other valuable natural elements as well as 'softer' political (great power) objectives.[142]

---

* "The western liberal notion of human rights, which is the basis for the UN Declaration of Human Rights, reduces the issues of the rights of human beings simply to preserving the civil liberties of individuals and provides a moral high ground for these rights to be imposed, by coercion, if necessary, on all non-western, and by definition illiberal, people."[140]

Bernard Hours, writing in Le Monde Diplomatique, identified a critical aspect of any consideration of the right to intervene, that is, the source of the mandate or authority to intervene and its supposed neutrality or non-political character: "Humanitarian aid workers claim they have a duty to intervene, and demand unrestricted access to victims. But ... this sort of intervention lacks political legitimacy. It presupposes that an imaginary global civil society gives a mandate to groups to intervene, and that these groups have no nationality, ideology or agenda of their own."[143] What Hours identifies is the kind of mystical aura of authority of human rights claims that puts them beyond question – or certainly beyond polite questioning.

Interventions in order to provide and deliver humanitarian aid, may, of course, be requested or encouraged by states in situations of natural disaster, such as drought or hurricanes, but in other situations the interventions may constitute a direct challenge to state sovereignty and authority, undertaken without invitation or consent of the state targeted. Humanitarian aid may also serve to relieve a government of its obligation to care for its own citizens.

At the same time, intervention in the affairs of another state may distract attention from situations and practices of aid organizations and state agencies in the home state, such as treatment of indigenous peoples within its own borders and broader issues of social and economic inequity.

While the source of the authority (the right) to intervene may be unclear or unspecified, the intervenor has no doubt about its power to intervene, which raises the question of accountability: in the words of Conor Foley, "To what extent can donors and international agencies impose their own 'rights-based' views on such societies without destroying local accountability?"[144] It would seem that the agencies and governments involved in such interventions have given little attention to this question.

The political equality of sovereign states was the foundation doctrine of the UN structure and embodied in its General Assembly. Since then, however, that equality has been replaced by a legal framework that prioritizes individual rights over state sovereignty, through the Universal Declaration of Human Rights and successive rights covenants. This evolution came about, says David Chandler, "because, on the one hand, the NGOs have either called for the politicization of aid or been complicit in its politicization, while, on the other hand, governments have sought to justify strategic policy-making through the ethical discourse of humanitarianism."[145] Chandler identifies the NATO assault on Kosovo in 1999 as the first internationally sanctioned military action in the name of human rights rather than international security. "In the Balkans, it was the intervening powers which defined the victim and prescribed the rights which they were choosing to uphold."[146] Conor Foley shares this concern about the politicalization of humanitarian aid: "Once they move away from the principles of neutrality and impartiality, it is also difficult to see how humanitarian agencies can ever be regarded as anything but political organizations."[147]

The increasing breadth and influence of the rights discourse in recent years, with its implicit moral imperatives and assumption of 'rightness', calls into question respect for the United Nations principle of state sovereignty, particularly for 'developing' countries, oppressive or dictatorial states, or what have come to be called failed and fragile states. Sovereignty becomes a state attribute on a selective basis – a Great Power prerogative. This becomes even more apparent in light of the increasing emphasis on the use of NATO for military intervention when the US and its allies cannot gain UN backing for their intended interventions.

There is no reason to regard national sovereignty as the ultimate in global governance, but if it, and the United

Nations, are to be undermined, consideration should be given to what might replace them. Clearly, during the period under discussion, the US, under George Bush, had visions of being *the* military and economic superpower in a unipolar world. The continuing expansion of NATO under the command of the traditional western Great Powers is a growing threat to the authority of the United Nations and should be addressed in the interests of global governance, peace and democracy.

It is ironic that in the years since Médecins sans Frontières was established, the United States of America has placed increasing emphasis on the sanctity and strength of its own borders while at the same time it has become the major violator of the national borders of others. 'Homeland security' has brought increasing insecurity to many individuals, peoples and states.

This radical (and cynical) disconnect between the stated values of the state and its actual practices at home and around the world was noted at an annual United Nations Conference in 2008 where discussion was described as being dominated by the sense that human rights have been globally weakened by the war between terrorism and counter-terrorism. "Immediately after September 11 we saw a dramatic change in government policies with regard to terrorism, suspected terrorism, and the monitoring of citizens, with the underlying assumption that human rights norms as established in conventions and treaties no longer apply."[148]

A good example of this may be the lack of state or private intervention to address the desperate conditions of the people of Zimbabwe. In this case, non-intervention suggests that this is due to the lack of significant oil reserves or valuable minerals – the state simply has no strategic or commercial value. At the same time there is massive intervention of all sorts in the Democratic Republic of the Congo, from the mining activities of transnational corporations and the financing of armed bands and militias to protect these interests, to humanitarian aid in an attempt to counter the violence and destructiveness of these activities. The actual role of ethnic rivalries is highly questionable, even though these are often cited as the cause of violence when in fact they may be the consequence of foreign commercial activities (interventions). Bernard Hours again: "The ideology of aid uses distress to mask injustice, and offers a meagre existence, little more than survival, where only the dying receive help.... Contrary to the aspirations of the Enlightenment, it legitimises the idea of a world divided between the successful and the weak."[149]

Clearly, some states are more sovereign than others. In the case of Zimbabwe, there might be an argument that the state has forfeited its legitimacy through its treatment of or disregard for its citizens. Such a judgement might appropriately be made by the UN General Assembly as the paramount international agency composed of all sovereign states.* One might make a similar argument concerning the state of Israel. Has it forfeited its legitimacy as a state through its treatment of the Palestinian people internally as well as in Gaza? In both cases, intervention might actually be more legitimate than not intervening in the name of respect for national sovereignty, but it certainly should not be assumed without public debate that there is a *de facto* right to intervene. Intervention might be authorized for a number of sound reasons, but that would still not make it a right; it would simply be a political decision.

The identity of those for whom humanitarian aid is intended or the 'victims' whose human rights are being 'abused', and who assigns them this identity, are crucial questions posed by assertion of the right to intervene.

---

* It has to be stressed that the UN is composed of all sovereign states, unlike bodies such as NATO or OECD that consist of *some* sovereign states but act as if they have as much as or more authority than the UN.

Bernard Hours provides a cogent analysis of the ideology of humanitarian aid and, by inference, human rights intervention. He identifies three principles on which the ideology of humanitarian aid depends: 1) universal human rights, "a worthy but problematic premise"; 2) the creation of victims you can save; 3) assertion of the right of access to these victims.

"Universal human rights ... make humanitarian aid legitimate. But who embodies these rights? Not the political citizen ... but a physical body who must be saved from famine, epidemics and natural disasters.... To what extent is the victim the subject of aid or the object? A victim's dignity is abstract, and depends on the situation (living in a refugee camp, for example). A human being has a status, but being a victim is merely a state. Victims are anonymous and interchangeable, passive players in the emotive campaign leaflets of NGOs. The relationship between rescuers and rescued is, by its nature, unequal.

"Most people do not see themselves as victims but as individuals confronting a crisis. Filipinos flattened by typhoons or Bangladeshis wading through floodwaters are dealing with a crisis which they see as part of their human destiny; they are dignified people living in a dangerous part of the world. It's others who see them as victims. Ambulances come only when you call them: aid agencies just turn up and declare an emergency. They save lives, but on their own terms."[150]

As I have argued, establishing a principle of human rights does not, in itself, entail actual fulfilment of the rights claims. The intervenors who seek to establish rights for others do not have any accompanying authority or responsibilities, which means that they may be able to claim high moral achievements without necessarily making any long-term difference in the lives of those identified as victims or being accountable to any authority (which returns us to the question of the origin of rights). Providing food for refugees in camps does not necessarily have anything to do with human rights; it is simply feeding the hungry for a time.

For the right to intervene to be transformed from an individualistic affair to improve or save the lives of individuals to a collective one – that is, a public intervention for the public collective good – institutional-structural change could well be required, radically changing the character of the intervention. What has actually happened in the past two decades, however, is something very different. Destruction of the infrastructure and institutional framework of a society in the name of providing humanitarian aid or protecting human rights is certainly the contradiction it appears to be.

There are other perspectives on the right to intervene. A report from the World Rainforest Movement explores the conditions that have led numerous forest peoples to voluntarily choose isolation. Brazilian Sydney Possuelo writes: "If we were more decent, there would be no peoples in isolation, but our behaviour has led them to seek protection from us. Their isolation is not voluntary, it is forced by us. These indigenous groups, because of their lifestyle, are self-sufficient in their own environment and – insofar as this is not altered – live in the abundance of what the forest gives them: hunting, fishing, fruit and timber combined with slash-and-burn farming, resources from the flora and fauna that their cultural practices and low demography allow to be renewable."[151]

Human rights and humanitarian aid are major components, and perhaps major rationalizations, of international affairs and global politics today. In this role, their history is brief, and it could well change again as bolder, more destructive and less apologetic regimes try to redefine state sovereignty. The long tradition of humanitarian

neutrality, embodied in the Red Cross, may come to be
sorely missed.

Is there, then, any intervention that is 'clean' and
legitimate?

The answer is probably 'no' as long as intervention
is, explicitly or implicitly, a police or military matter. MSF
was formed because some of its doctors felt that the
traditional neutrality of the International Committee of the
Red Cross was irresponsible. They felt, perhaps rightly, that
delivering humanitarian aid, whether in the form of medical
aid or food, while ignoring the context and causes of the
situation, was morally indefensible. A consequence of this
position, however, is what appears to be a growing
acceptance of military support to deliver aid and, in turn, the
direction of humanitarian aid by military forces.

"In December, 2008, US Agency for International
Development (USAID) and Department of Defense
(DoD) officials briefed international aid agencies in
Afghanistan on the new policy of the US government.
Titled 'Civilian-Military Cooperation Policy', it
spelled out that "it is USAID policy 'for all operating
units to cooperate with DoD in joint planning and
implementation ... in all aspects of foreign assistance
activities where both organizations are operating and
where civilian-military cooperation will advance US
Government foreign policy.' This means that DoD
will be able to create and enlarge its humanitarian programs and take a greater role in policy-making,
decisions and directives about the funding of security
assistance programs and humanitarian activities.
Elizabeth Ferris, of the Brookings Institution, adds
that "From channeling something like 4% of US over-
seas assistance a few years ago the military channeled
something like 22% of all US aid last year, which
means that rather than aid being seen as a response by

the US population to suffering people in need, it is increasingly seen as another tool of US foreign policy ... If US humanitarian NGOs refuse to work under these conditions, the [US government] can turn to for- profit contractors to provide the needed service without the bother of dealing with humanitarian principles."[152]

Behind this, we have to admit, is the very dangerous cultural arrogance and universalist assumption of the West. Does this reduce us to helplessness and despair? Not necessarily. Other cultures have other ways, and the ways of the west have not always been aggressive and violent. I remember living in Edinburgh and London when the police were unarmed. I also remember when United Nations blue-helmeted peacekeepers (including Canadians) sent to Korea in the mid-1950s were not military forces in the traditional sense, but were peacekeeping intervenors to whom one might have applied the medical ethic, "do no harm".

There is a cross-cultural tradition which seeks to intervene in order to defuse and avoid violence and actually reconcile conflicts. Ghandi was such an active intervenor. So was Jesus. So were the participants in the US civil rights movement of the 1950-60s and much of the anti-apartheid movement in South Africa. The power of such intervention is its ability to change the rules of the game, the relations of power. It is no longer an arms race because the intervenor refuses to bear arms. The intervenor is vulnerable and, in conventional terms, weak, powerless; but in that weakness is the moral strength of the intervenor.

A powerful learning for me was being one of a trio of students running a youth club in Greenside, a notorious slum of Edinburgh. The 'members' of the club were all the kids kicked out of every other facility in the city for causing trouble. Our single goal was to provide a safe place for them to meet and socialize without harassment by the police or anyone else. The ground rule was No Fighting. We spent a lot of our time intervening. Whenever we noticed an altercation brewing one of us would simply move slowly, with hands in pockets so that we offered no intimidation, and stand between the kids getting worked up. We never had a fight in the church hall. The police were never allowed in. The space belonged to the kids and they kept it that way.

One could even think that arms, the means of violence and destruction, are a measure of weakness, not of strength. For the police/military mind, it seems there is never enough: enough arms, enough fear. It is the creation of fear that generates bigger budgets for more militarization and more erosion, or outright destruction, of the fabric of society. Police and guns should not be synonymous. Police can be unarmed, or carry batons, and even pepper spray. However, technology is driving them in a more militaristic direction.

A photo of "an Afghan village elder with US soldiers on patrol" in the Indian news magazine Frontline caught my eye. The Afghan elder is in traditional robes with his bare left hand covering his mouth and chin. One of the US soldiers is in the foreground, fully clad in war-making gear, including automatic weapon. His hands are fully gloved. What kind of encounter can there be between the bare hand of an elder and the gloved hand of a foreign soldier?

Now we find police armed with 'non-lethal' stun guns ('tazers') enabling them to intervene from a safe distance and unmanned drones carrying electronically-guided bombs produce massive killing and destruction in Afghanistan while the intervenors remain safely in their fortresses.

The right to intervene has taken an evil turn.

WHERE WILL IT END?

In the years 1959-61, at the height of the Cold War, when I was studying theology and ethics with Reinhold Niebuhr, the leading intellectual of Christian realism at the time, there was no talk of human rights or humanitarian aid. International affairs were all about nuclear deterrence, lesser evil – 'your nuclear bomb is evil, ours is less evil because we have it just to deter you' – and great power politics. At the same time, there was little evidence of the individualism that has since redefined politics and put the individual and the individual's claim to rights ahead of the society in which he or she lives. While Niebuhr advocated a strong military and a policy of nuclear deterrence, he did recognize the legitimacy of a person standing on principle (a hallmark of the civil rights movement at that time) and even conscientious objection – the personal stance of refusing to participate in war or preparations for war, including military service.

While I was in seminary a small group of us traveled to Ft. Detrick, Maryland, for a weekend to join an ongoing 'intervention': a silent vigil outside the gate of the major chemical-biological warfare research facility in the USA. The vigil was led by an older Quaker couple who had been standing with their signs every day, for months, in silent protest against the activities of the facility. Every day the workers, as they drove in and out of their workplace, had to notice the vigil and its signs.

A personal stand, on principle, for what one believes against the demands of society and state, such as conscientious objection to military service, is a far cry from a claim against the state for rights of any kind, although one might work to have conscientious objection recognized by the state as a legitimate moral position coupled with alternative social or public health service.

In the post WWII years international affairs were dominated by the Cold War between the USSR and the USA and their respective allies and client states (1948-89). Events and developments in any country other than the USA were analyzed in relation to this great power polarization: you were for US or against US. Brutal Central and South American dictatorships were accepted as long as they were pro-capital and anti-communist. Stability and economic growth was the issue, not human welfare. As pointed out earlier, in this context dissidents in dictatorships found the language of human rights the only 'political' language they could speak, at least internationally.

It was only with the fall of the Berlin Wall in 1989 and the crumbling of the Soviet Union thereafter that space was created for recognition of other political and social issues. That same year the 'duty to intervene' was formulated; in the two decades since then, some of the international programs of humanitarian aid and human rights advocacy appear to have become uncomfortably closely allied with US commercial and strategic interests.

The past two decades have also been the era of rampant neoliberalism with its assumptions of universalism and evolutionary determinism. These assumptions have not been seen as hostile to human rights and so they have not been decisively rejected by human rights advocates.

The crumbling of the world as we have known it now requires that we reconsider the assumptions and framing of the concepts and practices of 'western civilization', including individualism, progress, property, capitalism and human rights. As the individualistic language of rights has assumed ever greater presence in our lives, social inequity has been growing and deepening. Neither legal entitlements nor economic growth will address this, stem its injustice, or lay the foundations for social justice and peace.

AFTERWORD

I write from the perspective of a culture that prefers monoculture, of all sorts, to diversity; a reductionist culture which seems to be troubled by contradictions, complexities and ambiguity; a culture which is eager to 'do something' to 'fix it'. A critic or dissenter is supposed to have straight-forward alternatives at hand, if not outright 'solutions' to the problems he or she raises with the status quo. What I have found interesting about the language of rights, however, is that in almost every case it neither calls for nor provides a meaningful solution to the subject of the claim. The language of rights remains an impotent juridical abstraction.

My preferred language would emphasize diversity and complexity, respect, responsibility and gratitude as characteristics not of what I am claiming of others, but of what I/we hope and intend to be and do. I don't consider this book a completed endeavour. It is, I hope, an invitation to continue a discussion and debate that has taken place as this book evolved. My own thinking has benefitted greatly by the reactions to my thesis and comments on drafts of various chapters by many people. A comment on one chapter from someone deeply involved in the issues discussed was what I hope for from many more readers: "I liked it very much, and found myself scribbling comments all over the manuscript – a sure sign that you have hit at least a few nerves!"

To facilitate comment and argument, *The Tyranny of Rights* is posted in full for free download (in 8½x11 format) at <http://ramshorn.ca/node/180>. The rights issue is global, and posting the book in this way also means that it can be passed around without restriction. Readers who have registered on the site and logged in are invited to post comments on the issues raised in the book.

My earlier books, *From Land to Mouth: Understanding the Food System*, and *Farmageddon: Food and the Culture of Biotechnology* are also available for free download at <www.ramshorn.ca>, and printed copies of *The Tyranny of Rights* in the standard paperback format can be ordered through this website as well.

REFERENCES

1. Radha D'Souza in *Seedling*, published by GRAIN, Barcelona, October 2007. Radha D'Souza teaches law at the University of Westminster, UK.

2. Judith Shklar, *Legalism – Law, Morals and Political Trials*, Harvard, 1964, p.10

3. Beauchamp & Childress, *Principles of Biomedical Ethics*, 3rd edition, Oxford, 1989, p.55. Thomas Hobbes is noted for his 1651 book of moral philosophy, *Leviathan*.

4. CORE, the Congress on Racial Equality, was one of the leading civil rights organizations in the 1960s. Since then it has become a right-wing black organization serving the interests of the drug and biotech industry.

5. Statement of the Pacific-Center Region of the *Congreso Nacional Indigena* meeting in Tlanixco state, Mexico, 25-26/1/03 (emphasis added)

6. Rights and Democracy, press release, 22/10/08

7. See Noam Chomsky, 'Humanitarian Imperialism: The New Doctrine of Imperial Right,' *Monthly Review*, September, 2008

8. "Dentist grits teeth..." Ottawa Citizen, 19/11/08

9. Kelly Eagan, Ottawa Citizen, 26/6/09

10. 'The Neocons' Ownership Society,' *Le Monde Diplomatique*, English edition, June 2005

11. Abby Lippman, Globe&Mail, 24/11/08

12. Ziauddin Sardar, *Postmodernism and the Other – The New Imperialism of Western Culture,* Pluto, 1998, pp.74-5

13. Richard Falk, *Frontline* (India) 27/3/09. Falk also suggests that Israel's attack on the civilian population of Gaza in early 2009 is "certainly a crime against humanity and a war crime," but that Israel is highly unlikely to be called before any

International Court of Justice, being one of the strong with impunity.

14. Don Buckingham, 'Food Security, Law and Theology: Biblical Underpinnings of the Right to Food, 2000', at: <http://donbuckingham.ca/CFGB.pdf>

15. *Ibid.* See also David Chandler, *From Kosovo to Kabul,* 2nd ed, Pluto, 2006

16. Guardian Weekly, 26/9/08

17. Esther Reed, *The Ethics of Human Rights*, Baylor University Press, 2007, p.23

18. Jurgen Habermas, *Time of Transitions*, Polity, 2006, p.155

19. David Harvey, *A Brief History of Neoliberalism*, Oxford, 2005, p.180

20. Indigenous National Congress, Central Pacific Region, *Declaration of Tuapurie*, 27/11/05

21. Timothy Mitchell, *Rule of Experts – Egypt, Techno-Politics, Modernity*, Univ. of California Press, 2002, p.54

22. *Ibid.*, p.55

23. Personal conversation

24. Farhad Mazhar, in 'What's Wrong with Rights', *Seedling,* published by GRAIN, Barcelona, October 2007

25. Robert Lovelace, retired chief, Airdock Algonquin First Nation, Ontario

26. Mustafa Koç, Ryerson University, Toronto

27. Zehra Arat, Purchase College, State University of New York

28. Personal communication, February 2008

29. *Le Monde diplomatique*, English edition, January 2009

30. Ziauddin Sardar, *Op. cit.*, p.68

31. *Ibid.*, p.70

32. See 'History of the Charter' at: <www.charterofrights.ca/en/ 26_00_01>. In 2009 the Government of Canada engaged in flagrant violation of the Charter in refusing to allow a Canadian citizen, Abousfian Abdelrazik, to return home from Sudan to Montreal until forced to do so by a court judgement.

33. "Pressure from provincial governments (which in Canada have jurisdiction over property) ... and from the country's left wing ... prevented Trudeau from including any rights protecting private property." <http://en.wikipedia.org/wiki/Canadian_Charter_of_ Rights _and_Freedoms>, accessed 14/7/09

34. For a provocative discussion, see Ugo Mattei and Laura Nader, *Plunder – When the Rule of Law is Illegal*, Blackwell, 2008

35. <www.unhchr.ch/html/menu3/b/a_ccpr.htm>

36. David Chandler, op. cit., p.92

37. Guardian Weekly, 13/2/09

38. Christopher Bickerton, 'Decoding Sarkozy', *Le Monde Diplomatique*, English edition, February 2009

39. Milan Kundera, in *Immortality,* quoted by Chandler, *op. cit.*, p.95

40. Sheldon Krimsky and Peter Shorett in *GeneWatch*, Council for Responsible Genetics, Jan-Feb. 2005 (emphasis added)

41. John Locke, *Second Treatise of Civil Government*, Ch 5, Sec 27, Of Property, <http://www.constitution.org/jl/2ndtr05.txt>

42. The concept/ideology of US past-President G.W. Bush's "Ownership Society" is attributed to John Locke by George Ross in an article about the Bush regime's plans for privatizing Social Security. See 'The Neocons' Ownership Society', *Le Monde Diplomatique*, English edition, June 2005

43. Sir William Blackstone, *Commentaries on the Laws of England*, Chap. I of Book I, first published in four volumes, 1765–1769

44. Jeffrey Kaplan, from Orion On-Line, www.oriononline.org/pages/om/03-6om/Kaplan.html

45. Marjorie Kelly, *The Divine Right of Capital*, Berrett-Koehler Publishers, 2001, p.203 note 23

46. Carol Rose, *Property and Persuasion*, Westview, 1994, p.2

47. Ottawa Citizen, 20/3/09

48. Ottawa Citizen, 10/4/09

49. For an incisive history of the social construction of the corporation, see David Noble, *Beyond the Promised Land*, Between the Lines, Toronto, 2005, chap.6

50. For a history of commodity creation and development in North America, see William Cronon, *Nature's Metropolis*, Norton, 1991

51. Graham Riches, *Right to Food Case Study: Canada*, 2004 (emphasis added)

52. United Nations Economic and Social Council, E/CN.4/2002/58, 10 January, 2002, Report by the Special Rapporteur on the right to food, Mr. Jean Ziegler

53. Resolution 2001/25

54. UN General Assembly, A/62/289, 22/8/07, Report of the Special Rapporteur on the Right to Food

55. 'Background Note: Analysis of the World Food Crisis by the U.N. Special Rapporteur on the Right to Food', Olivier de Schutter, 2/5/08

56. <www.world-governance.org/spip.php?article72>

57. 'B.C. Food Systems Network, Working Group on Indigenous Food Sovereignty, Final Activity Report,' prepared by Dawn Morrison, March, 2008

58. See: *Who Owns Nature?* ETCgroup, November 2008, at <www.etcgroup.org/en/materials/publications.html?pub _id=707>

59. See Stephen Jones, 'Breeding Resistance to Special Interests', at <www.bioscienceresource.org/docs/sjones-Breedingresistance.pdf>

60. Regine Andersen, *The History of Farmers' Rights*, Fridtjof Nansen Institute Report 8/2005, Oslo

61. Regine Andersen, *Protecting Farmers' Rights in the Global IPR Regime*, Policy Brief No 15, South Asia Watch on Trade, Economics & Environment (SAWTEE) 2007

62. Regine Andersen, *The History of Farmers' Rights*

63. See Devlin Kuyek, *Good Crop / Bad Crop – Seed Politics and the Future of Food in Canada*, Between the Lines, 2007

64. Regine Andersen, 'Summary of Findings from Phase 1, The Farmers' Rights Project', Oslo, 2006

65. *Protecting Farmers' Rights in the Global IPR Regime* - Policy Brief #15, 2007, prepared by Regine Andersen, for South Asia Watch on Trade, Economics & Environment (SAWTEE), Nepal

66. Drafted by the Traditional Native American Farmers' Association (TNAFA) and the New Mexico Acequia Association (NMAA) in January, February, and March 2006. <www.lasacequias.org/programs/seed-alliance/seed-declaration/>

67. Senate Joint Memorial 38, 2007

68. 'Call of the Earth/*Llamado de la Tierra* – an indigenous peoples' initiative on intellectual property policy – workshop outcomes,' Como, Italy, November 2003

69. 'Farmers' Rights in the International Treaty on Plant Genetic Resources for Food and Agriculture', <www.farmersrights.org/about/fr_in_itpgrfa.html> accessed 14/8/09

70. Personal comments of Marcelo Saavedra-Vargas, University of Ottawa

71. Michele Nori, Michael Taylor, Alessandra Sensi, 'Browsing on fences – Pastoral land rights, livelihoods and adaptation to climate change,' IIED issue paper no. 148, May 2008. See also Wm Cronon, *Changes in the Land – Indians, Colonists and the Ecology of New England,* Hill & Wang, 1983

72. *Ibid.*

73. Lungisile Ntsebeza, 'South Africa: Address the land question,' Mail and Guardian, Johannesburg, 19/8/07

74. Evangelina Robles, 'Territory and Property,' *Seedling,* GRAIN, October, 2007

75. *Ibid.*

76. *Ibid.*

77. Wm. Cronon, *op. cit.*

78. Bruce Chatwin, *The Songlines,* Penguin Books, 1987, p.5

79. See Hugh Brody, *Maps and Dreams,* Douglas & McIntyre, 1981, about mapping the territory of Canada's northwest in advance of oil exploration.

80. Indian and Northern Affairs Canada *Aboriginal title is based in history,* <www.ainc-inac.gc.ca/ai/mr/is/tcc-eng.asp>

81. BC Treaty Commission, *A Lay Person's Guide to Delgamuukw* – <www.bctreaty.net/files_3/pdf_documents/delgamuukw.pdf>

82. See 'Food crisis and the global land grab' at <http://farmlandgrab.org> for extensive coverage of this subject; also 'Food land grab puts world's poor at risk', Guardian Weekly, 10/7/09, p.12

83. Bruno Latour, *Politics of Nature,* Harvard, 2004, pp.155-6

84. Marjorie Kelly, op. cit., p.3

85. Globe&Mail, 2/1/09

86. Carol M. Rose, "Romans, Roads, and Romantic Creators: Traditions of Public Property in the Information Age" at

<www.law.duke.edu/journals/66LCPCarolRose> accessed 2/2/09

87. Karen Bakker, *Beyond Privatization: Water, Governance, Community*, Cornell, forthcoming

88. Karen Bakker, 'The Commons versus the Commodity', *Antipode*, 2007

89. *Frontline* (India), 14-27/7/07

90. globeandmail.com, 12/2/05

91. Reuters, 26/3/09

92. Bloomberg News, 27/6/06

93. Guardian Weekly, 20/3/03

94. Bloomberg News, 27/6/06

95. From an on-line investment newsletter, accessed 5/4/09

96. Karen Bakker, *Beyond Privatization*

97. Tom Regan, *The Case for Animal Rights*, California, 1983, 2004, p.xvii.

98. *Ibid.*, p.xvi

99. Bruno Latour, *op. cit.*, pp.76-79

100. Tom Regan, *op. cit.*, p.271

101. *Ibid.*, p.362

102. *Ibid.*, p.327

103. David Waltner-Toews, *One Animal Among Many – Gaia, Goats and Garlic*, NC Press, 1991

104. Donna Haraway, interview, *New Scientist*, 18/6/08

105. Passed by the Constituent Assembly, September 28, 2008

106. Community Environmental Legal Defense Fund, USA, Press Release, 28/9/08

107. For a detailed account of events surrounding this, see Raul Zibechi, 'Ecuador: The Logic of Development Clashes with Movements,' Americas Program Report (Washington, DC: Center for International Policy, March 17, 2009) at <http://americasprogram.org/am/5965>

108. Wall Street Journal, 10/10/0

109. <www.blauen-institut.ch/pg_blu/pa/aa.htm>

110. Actually, the first patent statute was the Venice decree of 1474, but the eclipse of Venice and the changing relations of power in Europe resulted in an unstable situation for intellectual property until the English Act of Anne in 1709.

111. Quoted by Andrew Kimbell in *The Human Body Shop*, Harper Collins, 1994, p.192

112. Geoff Tansey – "TRIPS with everything? Intellectual property and the farming world," A Food Ethics Council Report, 2002, p.35, quoting Peter Drahos

113. Christopher May, 'The hypocrisy of forgetfulness: The contemporary significance of early innovations in intellectual property', *Review of International Political Economy* 14:1 February 2007, 20

114. Carla Hesse, 'The rise of intellectual property, 700 B.C – A.D. 2000: an idea in the balance,' *Dædalus*, Spring, 2002, p.30

115. *Ibid.*, p.26

116. Carys Craig, 'Locke, Labour and Limiting the Author's Right: A Warning against a Lockean Approach to Copyright Law', *Queen's Law Journal* 28, 2002, p.15

117. *Ibid.*, p.54

118. "In the United States, individuals, not companies or institutions, must be named as inventors on patent applications. . . Most inventions are made in the context of the inventor's employment, and employees are typically required to assign to the employer all ownership rights in any invention

made on the job." – Sheiness & Canada in *Nature Biotechnology*, Feb 2006

119. May, C. and Sell, S., *Intellectual Property Rights: A Critical History*, Lynne Rienner Publishers, 2006, p.37

120. *Ibid.*, pp.17-19

121. *Ibid.*, p.20

122. Rainer Maria Rilke, *The Notebooks of Malte Laurids Brigge*, Norton, 1949 (completed in 1910)

123. For example, Amy Gutman, describing the position of rights advocate and Liberal politician Michael Ignatieff, says "The purpose of human rights, Ignatieff argues, is to protect human agency ... to treat people as purposive agents ... with a human life to lead." – Michael Ignatieff et al, *Human Rights*, Princeton, 2001, Amy Gutman, Introduction, pp.xviii-xx

124. Guy Brown, 'The Bitter End,' New Scientist 13/10/07

125. The U.N. special rapporteur for human rights in the occupied Palestinian territory, former Princeton University law professor Richard Falk, calls what Israel is doing to the 1.5 million Palestinians in Gaza "a crime against humanity". Falk, who is Jewish, has condemned the collective punishment of the Palestinians in Gaza as "a flagrant and massive violation of international humanitarian law as laid down in Article 33 of the Fourth Geneva Convention". He has asked for "the International Criminal Court to investigate the situation, and determine whether the Israeli civilian leaders and military commanders responsible for the Gaza siege should be indicted and prosecuted for violations of international criminal law." – Chris Hedges, *Israel's 'Crime Against Humanity'*, 16/12/08, <www.alternet.org/audits/113143/>

126. Currently familiar as a persona created by players in a video game.

127. <http://archives.cbc.ca/politics/rights_freedoms/topics/1135/>

128. New York Times, 3/12/08

129. Personal message from an "old and tired" friend

130. Jane Gross, 'The Immediate Cause of Death,' New York Times, 23/10/08

131. "Many procedures, especially in the final few weeks of a person's life, provide little benefit and bring little relief. Are we willing to set limits?" – Health Council of Canada, *Value for Money*, 2009

132. Eulogy for Jake Willems from his family, 2009, with permission

133. Address to the Nation, 7 October 2001, quoted by Conor Foley, *The Thin Blue Line*, Verso, 2008, p.110. See also James Orbinski, *An Imperfect Offering*, Doubleday Canada, 2008, pp.383-4

134. David Chandler, *op. cit.*, p.19, also James Orbinski, *op. cit.*, pp.383-4

135. Pierre Micheletti, 'World without Frontiers', *Le Monde diplomatique*, English edition, November, 2008

136. *Ibid.*

137. Caroline Fleuriot, 'A Right to intervene?', *Le Monde diplomatique*, English Edition, November, 2008

138. Bernard Kouchner, a founder of *Médecins sans Frontièrs*, Los Angeles Times, 18/10/99, quoted by David Chandler, *op. cit.*, p.57

139. Christopher Caldwell, in a review of *Le Monde selon K* by Pierre Péan, London Review of Books, 9/7/09.

140. James Orbinski, *op. cit.*, p.341

141. Ziauddin Sardar, *op. cit.*, p. 67

142. See 'The real agenda behind agricultural reconstruction in Afghanistan and Iraq' at <http://grain.org/briefings/?id+217>

143. Bernard Hours, 'NGOs and the victim industry', *Le Monde Diplomatique*, English edition, November 2008

144. Conor Foley, *op. cit.*, p.42

145. David Chandler, *op. cit.*, p.27

146. *Ibid.*, p.72

147. Conor Foley, *op. cit.*, p.16

148. Joanne Mariner of Human Rights Watch, United Nations Department of Public Information/Non-Governmental Organizations Conference, Paris, September, 2008,reported in 'Fighting the War on Terror', Inter Press Service News Agency, 8/9/08

149. Bernard Hours, *op. cit.*, 2008

150. *Ibid.*

151. 'Amazonia: The right of indigenous peoples to live in voluntary isolation,' World Rainforest Movement Bulletin #127, February, 2008

152. Huffington Post, 22/12/08